Antigone's Claim

THE WELLEK LIBRARY LECTURES

Irvine 2007

P9-DCG-906

The Breaking of the Vessels
Harold Bloom

In the Tracks of Historical Materialism
Perry Anderson

Forms of Attention
Frank Kermode

Memoires for Paul de Man
Jacques Derrida

The Ethics of Reading
J. Hillis Miller

Peregrinations: Law, Form, Event
Jean-François Lyotard

Reopening of Closure: Organicism Against Itself
Murray Krieger

Musical Elaborations
Edward W. Said

Three Steps on the Ladder of Writing
Hélène Cixous

The Seeds of Time
Fredric Jameson

Refiguring Life: Metaphors of Twentieth-Century Biology
Evelyn Fox Keller

A Fateful Question of Culture
Geoffrey Hartman

The Range of Interpretation
Wolfgang Iser

History's Disquiet: Modernity and Everyday Life
Harry Harootunian

The Vital Illusion
Jean Baudrillard

Death of a Discipline
Gayatri Chakravorty Spivak

Antigone's Claim

Kinship Between Life & Death

Judith Butler

COLUMBIA UNIVERSITY PRESS NEW YORK

COLUMBIA UNIVERSITY PRESS

PUBLISHERS SINCE 1893

NEW YORK   CHICHESTER, WEST SUSSEX

COPYRIGHT © 2000 COLUMBIA UNIVERSITY PRESS

LIBRARY OF CONGRESS CATALOGING-IN-PUBLICATION DATA

BUTLER, JUDITH P.

ANTIGONE'S CLAIM : KINSHIP BETWEEN LIFE AND DEATH /

JUDITH BUTLER.

P. CM. — (THE WELLEK LIBRARY LECTURES)

INCLUDES BIBLIOGRAPHICAL REFERENCES AND INDEX.

ISBN 0-231-11894-5 (CLOTH)

ISBN 0-231-11895-3 (PAPER)

1. ANTIGONE (GREEK MYTHOLOGY)   2. HEGEL, GEORG
WILHELM FRIEDRICH, 1770–1831.   3. IRIGARAY, LUCE.
4. LACAN, JACQUES, 1901–   5. KINSHIP—PHILOSOPHY.
6. FEMINIST THEORY. I. TITLE.   II. WELLEK LIBRARY LECTURE
SERIES AT THE UNIVERSITY OF CALIFORNIA, IRVINE.

B2948 .B855 2000

292.1'3—DC21

00–030321

∞

COLUMBIA UNIVERSITY PRESS BOOKS ARE
PRINTED ON PERMANENT AND DURABLE
ACID-FREE PAPER.
PRINTED IN THE UNITED STATES OF AMERICA
DESIGNED BY LISA HAMM
C 10 9 8 7 6 5 4 3 2
P 10 9 8 7 6 5 4 3

EDITORIAL NOTE

THE WELLEK LIBRARY LECTURES IN
CRITICAL THEORY ARE GIVEN ANNUALLY AT
THE UNIVERSITY OF CALIFORNIA, IRVINE,
UNDER THE AUSPICES OF
THE CRITICAL THEORY INSTITUTE.
THE FOLLOWING LECTURES WERE GIVEN
IN MAY 1998.

THE CRITICAL THEORY INSTITUTE
GABRIELE SCHWAB, DIRECTOR

Contents

Acknowledgments

These lectures were originally given as the Wellek Library Lectures at the University of California at Irvine in May 1998, the Messenger Lectures at Cornell University in September 1998, and the Christian Gauss Seminars at Princeton in November 1998. I am enormously grateful to the audiences on each of these occasions for their many helpful remarks. I would also like to thank the Guggenheim Foundation Fellowship for providing me with a fellowship to make substantial revisions of the manuscript in the spring of 1999. I also wish to thank, profoundly, Liana Theodoratou for her help with the Greek text and Mark Griffith for alerting me to the nuances of the play in its classical context and sharing with me an array of his rich scholarship on *Antigone*. Any mistakes in scholarship remain, of course, solely my own responsibility. I also thank Michael Wood for his engaged readings, Mark Poster for his important critical questions, Jonathan Culler for his ever valuable engagement with the work, Joan W. Scott for the provocations that come with enduring friendship, Drucilla Cornell for insisting on doing kinship otherwise, Wendy Brown for working through the fundamentals with me, Anna Tsing for deftly engaging an earlier version of the argument, and Bettina Mencke for her astute remarks on the project at the Einstein Forum in Berlin in June 1997. The students in the Berkeley Summer Research Institute in 1999 read all the primary texts covered here with wit, enthusiasm, and critical insight, as did the undergraduates in the senior Comparative Literature seminar on *Antigone* in the fall of 1998. I also thank the students and faculty in the Berkeley Summer Research Seminar in 1999 for their wonderful interpretations of the material. I thank especially Stuart Murray who helped with the final preparation in numerous important ways. His work has been invaluable to me. I also thank Anne Wagner for introducing me to the work of Ana Mendieta. And I thank Jennifer Crewe for her editorial patience. For their support, I thank Fran Bartkowski, Homi Bhabha, Eduardo Cadava, Michel Feher, Carla Freccero, Janet Halley, Gail Hershatter, Debra Keates, Biddy Martin, Ramona Naddaff, Denise Riley, and Kaja Silverman.

A Note on Translations

All translations from Sophocles' plays are from the Hugh Lloyd-Jones edition, published in the Loeb Library Series (Cambridge: Harvard University Press, 1994). On occasion, I also cite the David Grene translation, *Antigone* in *Sophocles I: Oedipus the King, Oedipus at Colonus, Antigone*, eds. David Grene and Richard Lattimore (Chicago: University of Chicago Press, 1991). All references after quotations from the plays are to line numbers.

They are gripped and shattered by something intrinsic to their own being.

—Hegel, *Aesthetics*

Antigone's Claim

CHAPTER 1
Antigone's Claim

I began to think about Antigone a few years ago as I wondered what happened to those feminist efforts to confront and defy the state. It seemed to me that Antigone might work as a counterfigure to the trend championed by recent feminists to seek the backing and authority of the state to implement feminist policy aims. The legacy of Antigone's defiance appeared to be lost in the contemporary efforts to recast political opposition as legal plaint and to seek the legitimacy of the state in the espousal of feminist claims. Indeed, one finds Antigone defended and championed, for instance, by Luce Irigaray as a principle of feminine defiance of statism and an example of anti-authoritarianism.[1]

But who is this "Antigone" that I sought to use as an example of a certain feminist impulse?[2] There is, of course, the "Antigone" of Sophocles' play by that name, and that Antigone is, after all, a fiction, one that does not easily allow itself to be made into an example one might follow without running the risk of slipping into irreality oneself. Not that this has stopped many people from making her into a representative of sorts. Hegel has her stand for the transition from matriarchal to patriarchal rule, but also for the principle of kinship. And Irigaray, though wavering on the representative function of Antigone, also insists upon it: "Her example is always worth reflecting upon as a historical figure and as an identity and identification for many girls and women living today. For this reflection, we must abstract Antigone from the seductive, reductive discourses and listen to what she has to say about government of the polis, its order and its laws" (*Speculum*, 70).

But can Antigone herself be made into a representative for a certain kind of feminist politics, if Antigone's own representative function is itself in crisis? As I hope to show in what follows, she hardly represents the normative principles of kinship, steeped as she is in incestuous legacies that confound her position within kinship. And she hardly represents a feminism that might in any way be unimplicated in the very power that it opposes. Indeed, it is not just that, as a fiction, the mimetic or representative character of Antigone is already put in question but that, as a figure for politics, she points somewhere else, not to politics as a question of representation but to that political possibility that emerges when the limits to representation and representability are exposed.

But let me recount my steps for you. I am no classicist and do not strive to be one. I read *Antigone* as many humanists have because the play poses questions about kinship and the state that recur in a number of cultural and historical contexts. I began to read Antigone and her critics to see if one could make a case for her exemplary political status as a feminine figure who defies the state through a powerful set of physical and linguistic acts. But I found something different from what I had anticipated. What struck me first was the way in which Antigone has been read by Hegel and Lacan and also by the way in which she has been taken up by Luce Irigaray and others[3] not as a political figure, one whose defiant speech has political implications, but rather as one who articulates a prepolitical opposition to politics, representing *kinship as the sphere that conditions the possibility of politics without ever entering into it*. Indeed, in the interpretation that Hegel has perhaps made most famous, and which continues to structure appropriations of the play within much literary theory and philosophical discourse, Antigone comes to represent kinship and its dissolution, and Creon comes to represent an emergent ethical order and state authority based on principles of universality.

What struck me second, however, is a point to which I hope to return toward the end of this chapter, which is the way that kinship is figured at the limit of what Hegel calls "the ethical order,"[4] the sphere of political participation but also of viable cultural norms, the sphere of legitimating *Sittlichkeit* (the articulated norms that govern the sphere of cultural intelligibility) in Hegelian terms. Within contemporary psychoanalytic theory, based on structuralist presuppositions and made perhaps most salient by the work of Jacques Lacan, this relation emerges in yet a different way. Lacan provides a reading of Antigone in his *Seminar VII*[5] in which she is understood to border the spheres of the imaginary and the symbolic and where she is understood, in fact, to figure the inauguration of the symbolic, the sphere of laws and norms that govern the accession to speech and speakability. This regulation takes place precisely through instantiating certain kin relations as symbolic norms.[6] As symbolic, these norms are not precisely social, and in this way Lacan departs from Hegel, we might say, by making a certain idealized notion of kinship into a presupposition of cultural intelligibility. At the same time Lacan continues a certain Hegelian legacy by separating that idealized sphere of kinship, the symbolic, from the sphere of the social. Hence, for Lacan, kinship is rarefied as enabling linguistic structure, a presupposition of symbolic intelligibility, and thus removed from the domain of the social; for Hegel, kinship is precisely a relation of "blood" rather than one of norms. That is, kinship is not yet entered into the social, where the social is inaugurated through a violent supersession of kinship.

The separation of kinship from the social haunts even the most anti-Hegelian positions within the structuralist legacy. For Irigaray, the insurrectionary power of Antigone is the power of that which remains outside the political; Antigone represents kinship and, indeed, the power of "blood" relations, which Irigaray doesn't mean in a precisely literal sense. For Irigaray, blood designates something of bodily specificity and graphicness that fully abstract principles of political equality not only fail to grasp but must rigorously exclude and even annihilate. Thus, by signifying "blood," Antigone does not precisely signify a blood *line* but something more like "bloodshed"—that which must be remaindered for authoritarian states to be maintained. The feminine, as it were, becomes this remainder, and "blood" becomes the graphic figure for this echoing trace of kinship, a refiguring of the figure of the bloodline that brings into relief the violent forgetting of primary kin relations in the inauguration of symbolic masculine authority. Antigone thus signifies for Irigaray the transition from the rule of law based on maternity, a rule of law based in kinship, to a rule of law based on paternity. But what precisely precludes the latter as kinship? There is the symbolic place of the mother that is taken over by the symbolic place of the father, but what has instituted those places to begin with? Is this not the same notion of kinship after all, with an accent and a value being placed on separate terms?

The context for Irigaray's reading is clearly Hegel's, who claims in *The Phenomenology of Spirit* that Antigone is "the eternal irony of the community." She is outside the terms of the polis, but she is, as it were, an outside without which the polis could not be. The ironies are no doubt more profound than Hegel understood: after all, she speaks, and speaks in public, precisely when she ought to be sequestered in the private domain. What sort of political speech is this that transgresses the very boundaries of the political, which sets into scandalous motion the boundary by which her speech ought to be contained? Hegel claims that Antigone represents the law of the household gods (conflating the chthonic gods of the Greek tradition with the Roman *Penates*) and that Creon represents the law of the state. He insists that the conflict between them is one in which kinship must give way to state authority as the final arbiter of justice. In other words, Antigone figures the threshold between kinship and the state, a transition in the *Phenomenology* that is not precisely an *Aufhebung*, for Antigone is surpassed without ever being preserved when ethical order emerges.

The Hegelian legacy of Antigone interpretation appears to assume the separability of kinship and the state, even as it posits an essential relation between them. And so every interpretive effort to cast a character as representative of kinship or the state tends to falter and lose coherence and stability.[7] This faltering has consequences not only for the effort to determine the representative function of any character but for the effort to think the relation between kinship and the state, a relation, I hope to show, that has relevance for us who read this play within a contemporary context in which the politics of kinship has brought a classical western dilemma into contemporary crisis. For two questions that the play poses are whether there can be kinship—and by kinship I do not mean the "family" in any specific form—without the support and mediation of the state, and whether there can be the state without the family as its support and mediation. And further, when kinship comes to pose a threat to state authority and the state sets itself in a violent struggle against kinship, can these very terms sustain their independence from one another? This becomes a textual problem of some importance as Antigone emerges in her criminality to speak in the name of politics and the law: she absorbs the very language of the state against which she rebels, and hers becomes a politics not of oppositional purity but of the scandalously impure.[8]

When I reread Sophocles' play, I was impressed in a perverse way by the blindnesses that afflict these very interpretations. Indeed, the blindnesses in the text—of the sentry, of Teiresias— seem invariably repeated in the partially blind readings of the text. Opposing Antigone to Creon as the encounter between the forces of kinship and those of state power fails to take into account the ways in which Antigone has already departed from kinship, herself the daughter of an incestuous bond, herself devoted to an impossible and death-bent incestuous love of her brother,[9] how her actions compel others to regard her as "manly" and thus cast doubt on the way that kinship might underwrite gender, how her language, paradoxically, most closely approximates Creon's, the language of sovereign authority and action, and how Creon himself assumes his sovereignty only by virtue of the kinship line that enables that succession, how he becomes, as it were, unmanned by Antigone's defiance, and finally by his own actions, at once abrogating the norms that secure his place in kinship and in sovereignty. Indeed, Sophocles' text makes clear that the two are metaphorically implicated in one another in ways that suggest that there is, in fact, no simple opposition between the two.[10] Moreover, to the extent that the two figures, Creon and Antigone, are chiasmically related, it appears that there is no easy separation between the two and that Antigone's power, to the extent that she still wields it for us, has to do not only with how kinship makes its claim within the language of the state but with *the social deformation of both idealized kinship and political sovereignty that emerges as a consequence of her act*. In her act, she transgresses both gender and kinship norms, and though the Hegelian tradition reads her fate as a sure sign that this transgression is necessarily failed and fatal, another reading is possible in which she exposes the socially contingent character of kinship, only to become the repeated occasion in the critical literature for a rewriting of that contingency as immutable necessity.

Antigone's crime, as you know, was to bury her brother after Creon, her uncle and the king, published an edict prohibiting such a burial. Her brother, Polyneices, leads an enemy army against his own brother's regime in Thebes in order to gain what he considers to be his rightful place as inheritor of the kingdom. Both Polyneices and his brother, Eteocles, die, whereupon Creon, the maternal uncle of the dead brothers, considers Polyneices an infidel and wants him denied a proper funeral, indeed, wants the body left bare, dishonored and ravaged.[11] Antigone acts, but what is her act? She buries her brother, indeed, she buries him twice, and the second time the guards report that they have seen her. When she appears before Creon, she acts again, this time verbally, refusing to deny that it was she who did the deed. In effect, what she refuses is the linguistic possibility of severing herself from the deed, but she does not assert it in any unambiguously affirmative way: she does not simply say, "I did the deed."

In fact, the deed itself seems to wander throughout the play, threatening to become attached to some doers, owned by some who could not have done it, disowned by others who might have done it. The act is everywhere delivered through speech acts: the guard reports that he has seen her; she reports that she has done it.

The only way that the doer is attached to the deed is through the linguistic assertion of the connection. Ismene claims that she will say that she did the deed, if Antigone will allow it, and Antigone refuses to allow it. The first time the sentry reports to Creon, he claims, "I did not do the deed, nor did I see who did" (25), as if to have seen it would have meant to have done it, or to have participated in its doing. He is aware that by reporting that he did see the deed, his very reporting will attach him to the deed, and he begs Creon to see the difference between the report of the deed and the deed itself. But the distinction is not only difficult for Creon to make, it survives as a fatal ambiguity in the text. The chorus speculates that "this action may have been prompted by the Gods" (29), apparently skeptical of its human authorship. And at the end of the play, Creon exclaims that the suicides of his wife and son are *his* acts, at which point the question of what it means to author a deed becomes fully ambiguous. Everyone seems aware that the deed is transferable from the doer, and yet, in the midst of the rhetorical proliferation of denials, Antigone asserts that she cannot deny that the deed is hers. Good enough. But can she affirm it?

Through what language does Antigone assume authorship of her act or, rather, refuse to deny that authorship? Antigone is introduced to us, you will remember, by the act by which she defies Creon's sovereignty, contesting the power of his edict, which is delivered as an imperative, one that has the power to do what it says, explicitly forbidding anyone to bury that body. Antigone thus marks the illocutionary failure of Creon's utterance, and her contestation takes the verbal form of a reassertion of sovereignty, refusing to dissociate the deed from her person: "I say that I did it and I do not deny it" (43), translated less literally by Grene as "Yes, I confess: I will not deny my deed" [in Greek, Creon says, "phes, e katarnei ne dedrakenai tade" and Antigone replies: "kai phemi drasai kouk aparnoumai to ne"].

"Yes, I confess it," or "I say I did it"—thus she answers a question that is posed to her from another authority, and thus she concedes the authority that this other has over her. "I will not deny my deed"—"I do not deny," I will not be forced into a denial, I will refuse to be forced into a denial by the other's language, and what I will not deny is my deed—a deed that becomes possessive, a grammatical possession that makes sense only within the context of the scene in which a forced confession is refused by her. In other words, to claim "I will not deny my deed" is to refuse to perform a denial, but it is not precisely to claim the act. To say, "Yes, I did it," is to claim the act, but it is also to commit another deed in the very claiming, the act of publishing one's deed, a new criminal venture that redoubles and takes the place of the old.

Interestingly enough, both Antigone's act of burial and her verbal defiance become the occasions on which she is called "manly" by the chorus, Creon, and the messengers.[12] Indeed, Creon, scandalized by her defiance, resolves that while he lives "no woman shall rule" (51), suggesting that if she rules, he will die. And at one point he angrily speaks to Haemon who has sided with Antigone and countered him: "Contemptible character, inferior to a woman!" (746). Earlier, he speaks his fear of becoming fully unmanned by her: if the powers that have done this deed go unpunished, "Now I am no man, but she the man [*aner*]" (528). Antigone thus appears to assume the form of a certain masculine sovereignty, a manhood that cannot be shared, which requires that its other be both feminine and inferior. But there is a question that persists: has she truly assumed this manhood? Has she crossed over into the gender of sovereignty?

This, of course, leads back to the question of how this manly and verbally defiant figure comes to stand for the gods of kinship. It strikes me as unclear whether Antigone represents kinship or, if she does, what sort of kinship it might be. At one point she appears to be obeying the gods, and Hegel insists that these are the gods of the household: she declares, of course, that she will not obey Creon's edict because it was not Zeus who published the law, thus claiming that Creon's authority is not Zeus's (496–501) and apparently displaying her faith in the law of the gods. And yet, she is hardly consistent on this score, noting in an infamous passage that she would not have done the same for other members of her family:

For never, had children of whom I was the mother or had my husband perished and been mouldering there would I have taken on myself this task, in defiance of the citizens. In virtue of what law do I say this? If my husband had died, I could have another, and a child by another man, if I had lost the first, but with my mother and father in Hades below, I could never have another brother. Such was the law for whose sake I did you special honour, but to Creon I seemed to do wrong and to show shocking recklessness, O my brother. And now he leads me thus by the hands, without marriage, without bridal, having no share in wedlock or in the rearing of children.   *(900–920)*

Antigone here hardly represents the sanctity of kinship, for it is for her brother or, at least, in his name, that she is willing to defy the law, although not for every kin. And though she claims to act in the name of a law that from Creon's perspective can appear only as a sanction for criminality, her law appears to have but one instance of application. Her brother is, in her view, not reproducible, but this means that the conditions under which the law becomes applicable are not reproducible. This is a law of the instant and, hence, a law with no generality and no transposability, one mired in the very circumstances to which it is applied, a law formulated precisely through the singular instance of its application and, therefore, no law at all in any ordinary, generalizable sense.

Thus she acts not in the name of the god of kinship but by transgressing the very mandates of those gods, a transgression that gives kinship its prohibitive and normative dimension but that also exposes its vulnerability. Although Hegel claims that her deed is opposed to Creon's, *the two acts mirror rather than oppose one another*, suggesting that if the one represents kinship and the other the state, they can perform this representation only by each becoming implicated in the idiom of the other. In speaking to him, she becomes manly; in being spoken to, he is unmanned, and so neither maintains their position within gender and the disturbance of kinship appears to destabilize gender throughout the play.

Antigone's deed is, in fact, ambiguous from the start, not only the defiant act in which she buries her brother but the verbal act in which she answers Creon's question; thus hers is an act in language. To publish one's act in language is in some sense the completion of the act, the moment as well that implicates her in the masculine excess called hubris. And so, as she begins to act in language, she also departs from herself. Her act is never fully her act, and though she uses language to claim her deed, to assert a "manly" and defiant autonomy, she can perform that act only through embodying the norms of the power she opposes. Indeed, what gives these verbal acts their power is the normative operation of power that they embody without quite becoming.

Antigone comes, then, to act in ways that are called manly not only because she acts in defiance of the law but also because she assumes the voice of the law in committing the act against the law. She not only does the deed, refusing to obey the edict, but she also does it again by refusing to deny that she has done it, thus appropriating the rhetoric of agency from Creon himself. Her agency emerges precisely through her refusal to honor his command, and yet the language of this refusal assimilates the very terms of sovereignty that she refuses. He expects that his word will govern her deeds, and she speaks back to him, countering his sovereign speech act by asserting her own sovereignty. The claiming becomes an act that reiterates the act it affirms, extending the act of insubordination by performing its avowal in language. This avowal, paradoxically, requires a sacrifice of autonomy at the very moment in which it is performed: she asserts herself through appropriating the voice of the other, the one to whom she is opposed; thus her autonomy is gained through the appropriation of the authoritative voice of the one she resists, an appropriation that has within it traces of a simultaneous refusal and assimilation of that very authority.[13]

In defying the state, she repeats as well the defiant act of her brother, thus offering a repetition of defiance that, in affirming her loyalty to her brother, situates her as the one who may substitute for him and, hence, replaces and territorializes him. She assumes manhood through vanquishing manhood, but she vanquishes it only by idealizing it. At one point her act appears to establish her rivalry and superiority to Polyneices: she asks, "And yet how could I have gained greater glory [*kleos*] than by placing my brother in his grave?" (502).

Not only does the state presuppose kinship and kinship presuppose the state but "acts" that are performed in the name of the one principle take place in the idiom of the other, confounding the distinction between the two at a rhetorical level and thus bringing into crisis the stability of the conceptual distinction between them.

Although I will return to Hegel and Lacan more comprehensively in the next chapter, it is helpful to see the various ways in which kinship, social order, and the state are variously, and sometimes inversely, figured in their texts. The state makes no appearance in Lacan's discussion of Antigone or, indeed, in Lévi-Strauss's early analysis of culture before him. A social order is based, rather, on a structure of communicability and intelligibility understood as symbolic. And though for both of these latter theorists, the symbolic is not nature, it nevertheless institutes the structure of kinship in ways that are not precisely malleable. For Hegel, kinship belongs to the sphere of cultural norms, but this sphere must be viewed in a subordinate relation to the state, even as the state is dependent on this structure of kinship for its own emergence and maintenance.

Thus Hegel can certainly acknowledge the way in which the state presupposes kinship relations, but he argues that the ideal is for the family to furnish young men for war, those who come to defend the boundaries of the nation, who come to confront one another in the life and death struggle of nations, and who ideally come to reside under a legal regime in which they are to some degree abstracted from the national *Sittlichkeit* that structures their participation.[14]

Antigone emerges as a figure for Hegel in the *Phenomenology* only to become transfigured and surpassed in the course of Hegel's description of what she does. For Hegel, however, Antigone passes away as the power of the feminine and becomes redefined as the power of the mother, one whose sole task within the travels of Spirit is to produce a son for the purposes of the state, a son who leaves the family in order to become a warring citizen. Thus *citizenship demands a partial repudiation of the kinship relations that bring the male citizen into being*, and yet kinship remains that which alone can produce male citizens.

Antigone finds no place within citizenship for Hegel because she is not capable of offering or receiving recognition within the ethical order.[15] The only kind of recognition she can enjoy (and here it is important to remember that recognition is, by definition in Hegel, reciprocal recognition) is of and by her brother. She can gain recognition only from the brother (and so therefore refuses to let him go) and because, according to Hegel, there is ostensibly no desire in that relationship. If there were desire in the relationship, there would be no possibility for recognition. But why?

Hegel does not tell us why, precisely, the ostensible lack of desire between brother and sister qualifies them for recognition within the terms of kinship, but his view implies that incest would constitute the impossibility of recognition, that the very scheme of cultural intelligibility, of *Sittlichkeit*, of the sphere in which reciprocal recognition is possible, presupposes the prepolitical stability of kinship. Implicitly, Hegel appears to understand that the prohibition against incest supports kinship, but this is not what he explicitly says. He claims, rather, that the "blood" relation makes desire impossible between sister and brother, and so it is the blood that stabilizes kinship and its internal dynamics of recognition. Thus Antigone does not desire her brother, according to Hegel, and so the *Phenomenology* becomes the textual instrument of the prohibition against incest, effecting what it cannot name, what it subsequently misnames through the figure of blood.

In fact, what is particularly odd is that in the earlier discussion of recognition in the *Phenomenology*, desire (¶ 167) becomes the desire for recognition, a desire that seeks its reflection in the Other, a desire that seeks to negate the alterity of the Other, a desire that finds itself in the bind of requiring the Other whom one fears to be and to be captured by; indeed, without this constituting passionate bind, there can be no recognition. In that earlier discussion, the drama of reciprocal recognition begins when one consciousness finds that it is lost, lost in the Other, that it has come outside itself, that it finds itself as the Other or, indeed, in the Other. Thus recognition begins with the insight that one is lost in the Other, appropriated in and by an alterity that is and is not oneself, and recognition is motivated by the desire to find oneself reflected there, where the reflection is not a final expropriation. Indeed, consciousness seeks a retrieval of itself, only to recognize that there is no return from alterity to a former self but only a transfiguration premised on the impossibility of return.

Thus in "Lordship and Bondage" recognition is motivated by the desire for recognition, and recognition is itself a cultivated form of desire, no longer the simple consumption or negation of alterity but the uneasy dynamic in which one seeks to find oneself in the Other only to find that this reflection is the sign of one's expropriation and self-loss. Thus in the earlier section, for the subject of the *Phenomenology*, there is no recognition without desire. And yet, for Antigone, according to Hegel, there can be no recognition with desire. Indeed, there is for her recognition only within the sphere of kinship, and with her brother, on the condition that there is no desire.

Lacan's reading of Antigone, to which I will return in the following chapter, also suggests that there is a certain ideality to kinship and that Antigone offers us access to this symbolic position. It is not the content of her brother, Lacan claims, that she loves, but his "pure Being," an ideality of being that belongs to symbolic positions. The symbolic is secured precisely through an evacuation or negation of the living person; thus a symbolic position is never commensurate with any individual who happens to occupy it; it assumes its status as symbolic precisely as a function of that incommensurability.

Thus Lacan presupposes that the brother exists at a symbolic level and that this symbolic brother is the one whom Antigone loves. Lacanians tend to sever the symbolic account of kinship from the social, thus freezing the social arrangements of kinship as something intact and intractable, as that which social theory might do in a different register and at a different time. Such views sever the social and the symbolic only to retain an invariant sense of kinship in the latter. The symbolic, which gives us kinship as a function of language, is separated from the social arrangements of kinship, presupposing that (a) kinship is instituted at the moment that the child accedes to language, (b) kinship is a function of language rather than any socially alterable institution, and (c) language and kinship are not socially alterable institutions—at least, not easily altered.

So Antigone, who from Hegel through Lacan is said to defend kinship, a kinship that is markedly *not* social, a kinship that follows rules that are the condition of intelligibility for the social, nevertheless represents, as it were, kinship's fatal aberration. Lévi-Strauss remarks upon the interiority of the rules governing kinship when he writes that "the fact of being a rule, completely independent of its modalities, is indeed the very essence of the incest prohibition" (32, 37).[16] Thus it is not simply that the prohibition is such a rule but that this prohibition instantiates the ideality and persistence of the rule itself. "The rule," he writes, "is at once social, in that it is a rule, and *pre-social*, in its *universality* and the *type* of relationships on which it imposes its norm" (12, 14). And later he maintains that the incest taboo is not exclusively biological (although partially), nor exclusively cultural, but exists rather "at the threshold of culture," part of a set of rules that generate the possibility of culture and are thus distinct from the culture they generate, but not absolutely.

In the chapter entitled "The Problem of Incest," Lévi-Strauss makes clear that the set of rules he is articulating are, strictly speaking, neither biological nor cultural. He writes, "It is true that, through its universality, the prohibition of incest touches upon nature [touche à la nature], i.e., upon biology or psychology, or both. But it is just as certain [il n'est pas moins certain] that in being a rule it is a social phenomenon, and belongs to the world of rules [l'univers des règles], hence to culture, and to sociology, whose study is culture" (24, 28). Explaining the consequences, then, for a viable ethnology, Lévi-Strauss maintains that one must acknowledge "the one pre-eminent and universal rule which assures culture's hold over nature [la Règle par excellence, la seule universelle et qui assure la prise de la culture sur la nature]" (24, 28). Lévi-Strauss makes clear how difficult it is to determine the status of this universal prohibition further along in this same discussion when he writes,

> The prohibition of incest is in origin neither purely cultural nor purely natural, nor is it a composite mixture of elements from both nature and culture. It is the fundamental step [la démarche fondamentale] because of which, by which, but above all in which, the transition from nature to culture is accomplished. In one sense, it belongs to nature, for it is a general condition of culture. Consequently, we should not be surprised that its formal characteristic, universality, has been taken from nature [tenir de la nature]. However, in another sense, it is already culture, exercising and imposing its rule on phenomena which initially are not subject to it.   (24, 28–29)

Although Lévi-Strauss insists that the prohibition is neither the one (nature) nor the other (culture), he also proposes to think of the prohibition as the "link [*le lien*]" between the one and the other. But if it is a relation of mutual exclusion, it is difficult to understand it as a link or, indeed, a transition.[17] And so it seems that his text vacillates between these various positions, understanding the rule as partially composed of nature and culture, but not exclusively, understanding it as exclusive of both categories, understanding it as the transition, sometimes understood as causal, or the link, sometimes understood as structural, between nature and culture.

The Elementary Structures of Kinship was published in 1947, and within six years Lacan began to develop his more systematic account of the symbolic, those threshold rules that make culture possible and intelligible, which are neither fully reducible to their social character nor permanently divorced from the social. One question that will be pursued in the succeeding chapters is whether one might critically assess the status of these rules that govern cultural intelligibility but are not reducible to a given culture. Moreover, how do such rules work? On the one hand, we are told that the rule of prohibiting incest is universal, but Lévi-Strauss also acknowledges that it does not always "work." What he does not pursue, however, is the question, what forms does its nonworking take? Moreover, when the prohibition appears to work, does it have to sustain and manage a specter of its nonworking in order to proceed?

More specifically, can such a rule, understood as a prohibition, actually operate, however effectively, without producing and maintaining the specter of its transgression? Do such rules produce conformity, or do they also produce a set of social configurations that exceed and defy the rules by which they are occasioned? I take this question to be what Foucault has underlined as the *productive* and *excessive* dimension of the rules of structuralism. To accept the final efficacy of the rule in one's theoretical descriptions is thus to live under its regime, accept the force of its edict, as it were. How interesting, then, that so many of the readings of Sophocles' play insist that there is no incestuous love here, and one wonders whether the reading of the play does not in those instances become the very occasion for the insistence of the rule to take place: there is no incest here, and cannot be.[18] Hegel makes the most dramatic of such gestures when he insists that there is only absence of desire between brother and sister. Even Martha Nussbaum in her reflections on the play remarks that Antigone appears to have no great attachment to the brother.[19] And Lacan claims of course that it is not the brother *in his content* whom she loves, but his being as such—but where does that leave us? What kind of place or position is this? For Lacan, Antigone pursues a desire that can only lead to death precisely because it

seeks to defy symbolic norms. But is this the right way to inter-
pret her desire? Or has the symbolic itself produced a crisis for its
own intelligibility? Can we assume that Antigone has no confu-
sion about who is her brother, and who is her father, that
Antigone is not, as it were, living the equivocations that unravel
the purity and universality of those structuralist rules?

Lacanian theorists for the most part insist that symbolic norms
are not the same as social ones. The "symbolic" becomes a tech-
nical term for Lacan in 1953 and becomes his own way of com-
pounding mathematical (formal) and Lévi-Straussian uses of the
term. The symbolic is defined as the realm of the Law that regu-
lates desire in the Oedipus complex.[20] That complex is understood to be derived from a primary or symbolic prohibition
against incest, a prohibition that makes sense only in terms of kinship relations in which various "positions" are established within
the family according to an exogamic mandate. In other words, a
mother is someone with whom a son and daughter do not have
sexual relations, and a father is someone with whom a son and
daughter do not have sexual relations, a mother is someone who
only has sexual relations with the father, etc. These relations of
prohibition are thus encoded in the "position" that each of these
family members occupies. To be in such a position is thus to be in
such a crossed sexual relation, at least according to the symbolic
or normative conception of what that "position" is.

The structuralist legacy within psychoanalytic thinking has
exerted a significant influence on feminist film and literary theory,
as well as feminist approaches to psychoanalysis throughout the
disciplines. Indeed, we hear a great deal of "position" talk within
recent cultural theory, and are not always aware of its genesis. It
also paved the way for a queer critique of feminism that has had,
and continues to have, divisive and productive effects within sexuality and gender studies. From this perspective, we ask, Is there
a social life left for kinship, one that might well accommodate
change within kinship relations? For anyone working within con-

temporary gender and sexuality studies, the task is not easy, given the legacy of theoretical work that derives from this structuralist paradigm and its Hegelian precursors.

My view is that the distinction between symbolic and social law cannot finally hold, that not only is the symbolic itself the sedimentation of social practices but that radical alterations in kinship demand a rearticulation of the structuralist presuppositions of psychoanalysis and, hence, of contemporary gender and sexual theory.

With this task in mind, we return to the scene of the incest taboo, where the question emerges: What is the status of these prohibitions and these positions? Lévi-Strauss makes clear in *The Elementary Structures of Kinship* that nothing in biology necessitates the incest taboo, that it is the mechanism by which biology is transformed into culture, and so is neither biological nor cultural, although culture itself cannot do without it. By "cultural," Lévi-Strauss does not mean "culturally variable" or "contingent," but rather, operating according to "universal" rules of culture. Thus, for Lévi-Strauss, cultural rules are not alterable rules (as Gayle Rubin subsequently argued), but the modalities in which they appear are variable. Moreover, these rules are what operate to transform biological relations into culture, but they belong to no specific culture. No specific culture can come into being without them, but they are irreducible to any of the cultures that they bring into being. The domain of a universal and eternal rule of culture, what Juliet Mitchell called "the universal and primordial law,"[21] becomes the basis for the Lacanian notion of the symbolic and the subsequent efforts to separate the symbolic both from the spheres of biology and the social.

In Lacan, that which is universal in culture is understood to be its symbolic or linguistic rules, and these are understood to encode and support kinship relations. The very possibility of pronomial reference, of an "I" a "you" a "we" and "they," appears to rely on this mode of kinship that operates in and as language.

This slide from the cultural to the linguistic is one toward which Lévi-Strauss himself gestures near the end of *The Elementary Structures of Kinship*. In Lacan the symbolic becomes defined in terms of a conception of linguistic structures that are irreducible to the social forms that language takes or that, according to structuralist terms, might be said to establish the universal conditions under which the sociality, i.e., the communicability of all language use, becomes possible. This move paves the way for the consequential distinction between symbolic and social accounts of kinship.

Hence a social norm is not quite the same as a "symbolic position" in the Lacanian sense, which appears to enjoy a quasi-timeless character, regardless of the qualifications offered in endnotes to various of the master's seminars. Lacanians almost always insist that it would be a mistake to take the symbolic position of the father, for instance, which is after all the paradigmatically symbolic position, and mistake that for a socially constituted and alterable position that fathers have assumed through time. The Lacanian view insists that there is an ideal and unconscious demand made upon social life irreducible to socially legible causes and effects. The symbolic place of the father does not cede to the demands for a social reorganization of paternity. The symbolic is precisely what sets limits to any and all utopian efforts to reconfigure and relive kinship relations at some distance from the oedipal scene.[22]

When the study of kinship was combined with the study of structural linguistics, kinship positions were elevated to the status of a certain order of linguistic positions without which no signification could proceed, no intelligibility could be possible. What were the consequences of making certain conceptions of kinship timeless and then elevating them to the status of the elementary structures of intelligibility? Is this any better or worse than postulating kinship as a natural form?

So if a social norm is not the same as a symbolic position, then a symbolic position, here understood as the sedimented ideality of the norm, appears to depart from itself. The distinction between them does not quite hold, for in each instance we are still referring to social norms, but in different modes of appearance. The ideal form is still a contingent norm, but one whose contingency has been rendered necessary, a form of reification with stark consequences for gendered life. Those who disagree with me tend to claim, with some exasperation, "But it is the law!" But what is the status of such an utterance? "It is the law!" becomes the utterance that performatively attributes the very force to the law that the law itself is said to exercise. "It is the law" is thus a sign of allegiance to the law, a sign of the desire for the law to be the indisputable law, a theological impulse within the theory of psychoanalysis that seeks to put out of play any criticism of the symbolic father, the law of psychoanalysis itself. Thus the status given to the law is precisely the status given to the phallus, the symbolic place of the father, the indisputable and incontestable. The theory exposes its own tautological defense. The law beyond laws will finally put an end to the anxiety produced by a critical relation to final authority that clearly does not know when to stop: a limit to the social, the subversive, the possibility of agency and change, a limit that we cling to, symptomatically, as the final defeat of our own power. Its defenders claim that to be without such a law is pure voluntarism or radical anarchy! Or is it? And to accept such a law as a final arbiter of kinship life? Is that not to resolve by theological means the concrete dilemmas of human sexual arrangements that have no ultimate normative form?

One can certainly concede that desire is radically conditioned without claiming that it is radically determined, and that there are structures that make possible desire without claiming that those structures are impervious to a reiterative and transformative articulation. The latter is hardly a return to "the ego" or classical liberal notions of freedom, but it does insist that the norm has a temporality that opens it to a subversion from within and to a future that cannot be fully anticipated. And yet, Antigone cannot quite stand for that subversion and for that future, because what she draws into crisis is the representative function itself, the very horizon of intelligibility in which she operates and according to which she remains somewhat unthinkable. Antigone is the offspring of Oedipus and so raises the question for us: what will come of the inheritance of Oedipus when the rules that Oedipus blindly defies and institutes no longer carry the stability accorded to them by Lévi-Strauss and structural psychoanalysis? In other words, Antigone is one for whom symbolic positions have become incoherent, confounding as she does brother and father, emerging as she does not as a mother but—as one etymology suggests—"in the place of the mother."[23] Her name is also construed as "antigeneration" (*gonē* [generation]).[24] She is, thus, already at a distance from that which she represents, and what she represents is far from clear. If the stability of the maternal place cannot be secured, and neither can the stability of the paternal, what happens to Oedipus and the interdiction for which he stands? What has Oedipus engendered?

I ask this question, of course, during a time in which the family is at once idealized in nostalgic ways within various cultural forms, a time in which the Vatican protests against homosexuality not only as an assault on the family but also on the notion of the human, where to become human, for some, requires participation in the family in its normative sense. I ask this as well during a time in which children, because of divorce and remarriage, because of migration, exile, and refugee status, because of global displacements of various kinds, move from one family to another, move from a family to no family, move from no family to a family, or in which they live, psychically, at the crossroads of the family, or in multiply layered family situations, in which they may well have more than one woman who operates as the mother, more than one man who operates as the father, or no mother or no father, with half-brothers who are also friends—this is a time in which kinship has become fragile, porous, and expansive. It is also a time in which straight and gay families are sometimes blended, or in which gay families emerge in nuclear and non-nuclear forms. What will the legacy of Oedipus be for those who are formed in these situations, where positions are hardly clear, where the place of the father is dispersed, where the place of the mother is multiply occupied or displaced, where the symbolic in its stasis no longer holds?

In some ways Antigone figures the limits of intelligibility exposed at the limits of kinship. But she does it in a way that is hardly pure, and that will be difficult for anyone to romanticize or, indeed, to consult as an example. After all, Antigone appropriates the stance and idiom of the one she opposes, assumes Creon's sovereignty, even claims the glory that is destined for her brother, and lives out a strange loyalty to her father, bound as she is to him through his curse. Her fate is not to have a life to live, to be condemned to death prior to any possibility of life. This raises the question of how it is that kinship secures the conditions of intelligibility by which life becomes livable, by which life also becomes condemned and foreclosed. Antigone's death is always double throughout the play: she claims that she has not lived, that she has not loved, and that she has not borne children, and so that she has been under the curse that Oedipus laid upon his children, "serving death" for the length of her life. Thus death signifies the unlived life, and so as she approaches the living tomb that Creon has arranged for her, she meets a fate that has been hers all along. Is it perhaps the unlivable desire with which she lives, incest itself, that makes of her life a living death, that has no place within the terms that confer intelligibility on life? As she approaches the tomb, where she must remain entombed in life, she remarks,

O tomb, O bridal chamber, O deep-dug home, to be guarded for ever, where I go to join those who are my own [tous emautes]. *(891–893)*

Thus death is figured as a kind of marriage to those in her family who are already dead, affirming the deathlike quality of those loves for which there is no viable and livable place in culture. It is no doubt important, on the one hand, to refuse her conclusion that to be without a child is itself a tragic fate, and, on the other hand, to refuse the conclusion that the incest taboo must be undone in order for love to freely flourish everywhere. Neither the return to familial normalcy nor the celebration of incestuous practice is here the aim. Her predicament, though, does offer an allegory for the crisis of kinship: which social arrangements can be recognized as legitimate love, and which human losses can be explicitly grieved as real and consequential loss? Antigone refuses to obey any law that refuses public recognition of her loss, and in this way prefigures the situation that those with publicly ungrievable losses—from AIDS, for instance—know too well. To what sort of living death have they been condemned?

Although Antigone dies, her deed remains in language, but what is her deed? This deed *is* and *is not* her own, a trespass on the norms of kinship and gender that exposes the precarious character of those norms, their sudden and disturbing transferability, and their capacity to be reiterated in contexts and in ways that are not fully to be anticipated.

Antigone represents not kinship in its ideal form but its deformation and displacement, one that puts the reigning regimes of representation into crisis and raises the question of what the conditions of intelligibility could have been that would have made her life possible, indeed, what sustaining web of relations makes our lives possible, those of us who confound kinship in the rearticulation of its terms? What new schemes of intelligibility make our loves legitimate and recognizable, our losses true losses? This question reopens the relation between kinship and reigning epistemes of cultural intelligibility, and both of these to the possibility of social transformation. And this question, which seems so hard to ask when it comes to kinship, is so quickly suppressed by those who seek to make normative versions of kinship essential to the working of culture and the logic of things, a question too often foreclosed by those who, from terror, savor the final authority of those taboos that stabilize social structure as timeless truth, without then ever asking, what happened to the heirs of Oedipus?

CHAPTER 2

Unwritten Laws, Aberrant Transmissions

In the last chapter, I considered Antigone's act, what claim the act of burial makes, what act the claim of defiance performs. Her act leads to her death, but the relationship between the act and her fatal conclusion is not precisely causal. She acts, she defies the law, knowing that death is the punishment, but what propels her action? And what propels her action toward death? It would be easier if we could say that Creon killed her, but Creon banishes her only to a living death, and it is within that tomb that she takes her life. It might be possible to say that she authors her own death, but what legacy of acts is being worked out through the instrument of her agency? Is her fatality a necessity? And if not, under what non-necessary conditions does her fatality come to appear as necessity?

She attempts to speak in the political sphere in the language of sovereignty that is the instrument of political power. Creon makes his proclamation and asks that his guards make sure that everyone knows his words. "These are the rules by which I make our city great" (190), and yet his enunciation is not enough. He must ask the guards to transmit his proclamation, and one of them balks: "Give this burden to some younger man to carry!" (216).

As the play begins, it turns out that Ismene has not heard the proclamation that Antigone reports "Creon has made to the whole city" (7), and so it appears that Creon's sovereign act of speech depends upon its reception and transmission by his subordinates for its power: it can fall on deaf or resistant ears and thus fail to bind those to whom it is addressed. What is clear, however, is that Creon *wants* his word to be known and honored by the entire polis. Similarly, Antigone does not shrink from the possibility of having her defiance known. When Ismene counsels her early in the play, "Tell no one of this act beforehand" (84), Antigone responds, "Ah, tell them all! I shall hate you far more if you remain silent, and do not proclaim this to all" (86–87). Like Creon, then, Antigone wants her speech act to be radically and comprehensively public, as public as the edict itself.

Although her defiance is heard, the price of her speech is death. Her language is not that of a survivable political agency. Her words, understood as deeds, are chiasmically related to the vernacular of sovereign power, speaking in and against it, delivering and defying imperatives at the same time, inhabiting the language of sovereignty at the very moment in which she opposes sovereign power and is excluded from its terms. What this suggests is that she cannot make her claim outside the language of the state, but neither can the claim she wants to make be fully assimilated by the state.[1]

But if her actions are not politically survivable ones, they reside no less unproblematically within the sphere of kinship. As if troubled by the very deformation of kinship that she performs and portends, critics of the play have responded with an idealization of kinship that denies the challenge that is being made against it. There are two forms of idealized kinship to be considered here: one she is said to support through representing its terms, another she is understood to support through constituting its limit. The first is Hegel's who has Antigone represent the laws of kinship, the household gods, a representation that leads to two strange consequences: one, that her insistence, according to him, on representing those laws is precisely what constitutes a crime in another more public order of law, and two, that she who stands for this feminine domain of the household becomes unnameable within the text, that the very representation she is said to enact requires an effacement of her name in the text of *The Phenomenology of Spirit*. The second is Lacan's who establishes Antigone at the threshold of the symbolic, understood as the linguistic register in which kinship relations are instated and maintained; he understands her death as precipitated precisely by the symbolic insupportability of her desire. Although I take my distance from both of these consequential readings, I am also endeavoring to rework aspects of both positions in the account that I provide to these questions: Does Antigone's death signal a necessary lesson about the limits of cultural intelligibility, the limits of intelligible kinship, one that restores us to our proper sense of limit and constraint? Does Antigone's death signal the supersession of kinship by the state, the necessary subordination of the former to the latter? Or is her death precisely a limit that requires to be read as that operation of political power that forecloses what forms of kinship will be intelligible, what kinds of lives can be countenanced as living?

In Hegel, kinship is rigorously distinguished from the sphere of the state, though kinship is a precondition for the emergence and reproduction of the state apparatus. In Lacan, kinship, as a function of the symbolic, becomes rigorously dissociated from the sphere of the social, and yet it constitutes the structural field of intelligibility within which the social emerges. My reading of Antigone, in brief, will attempt to compel these distinctions into productive crisis. Antigone represents neither kinship nor its radical outside but becomes the occasion for a reading of a structurally constrained notion of kinship in terms of its social iterability, the aberrant temporality of the norm.

To recast positions of kinship as "symbolic" is precisely to posit them as preconditions of linguistic communicability and to suggest that these "positions" bear an intractability that does not apply to contingent social norms. It is, however, not enough to trace the effects of social norms on the thinking of kinship, a move that would return the discourse on kinship to a sociologism devoid of psychic significance. Norms do not unilaterally act upon the psyche; rather, they become condensed as the figure of the law to which the psyche returns. The psychic relation to social norms can, under certain conditions, posit those norms as intractable, punitive, and eternal, but that figuration of norms already takes place within what Freud called "the culture of the death drive." In other words, the very description of the symbolic as intractable law takes place within a fantasy of law as insurpassable authority. In my view, Lacan at once analyzes and symptomizes this fantasy. I hope to suggest that the notion of the symbolic is limited by the description of its own transcendentalizing function, that it can acknowledge the contingency of its own structure only by disavowing the possibility of any substantial alteration in its field of operation. My suggestion will be that the relation between symbolic position and social norm needs to be rethought, and in my final chapter, I hope to show how one might reapproach the kinship-founding function of the incest taboo within psychoanalysis with a conception of a contingent social norm at work. Here I am less interested in what the taboo constrains than the forms of kinship to which it gives rise and how their legitimacy is established precisely as the normalized solutions to the oedipal crisis. The point, then, is not to unleash incest from its constraints but to ask what forms of normative kinship are understood to proceed as structural necessities from that taboo.

Antigone is only partially outside the law, and so one might conclude that neither the law of kinship nor the law of the state works effectively to order the individuals who are subject to these laws. But if her deviance is used to illustrate the inexorability of the law and its dialectical opposition, then her opposition works in the service of the law, shoring up its inevitability.

I propose to consider two such instances in which Antigone is understood to occupy a position anterior to the state and anterior to kinship in order to determine where she stands, how she acts, and in the name of what. The first set of instances is to be found in Hegel's discussion in *The Phenomenology of Spirit* and *The Philosophy of Right*, and the second, which I consider in the next chapter, is the seventh seminar of Jacques Lacan devoted to the topic of "The Ethics of Psychoanalysis."

Hegel approaches the status of Antigone in the chapter of the *Phenomenology* entitled "The Ethical Life," in a subsection called "Ethical Action: Human and Divine Knowledge, Guilt and Destiny" [Die Sittliche Handlung: Das Menschliche und Göttliche Wissen, die Schuld und das Schicksal].[2] In fact, she remains largely unnamed in this section, merely prefigured through most of the discussion. Hegel interrogates the place of guilt and crime in universal ethical life and insists that, within this sphere, when one acts criminally one does not act as an individual, for one becomes an individual only on the condition that one belongs to community. Ethical life is precisely a life structured by *Sittlichkeit*, where the norms of social intelligibility are historically and socially produced.[3] The self who acts, and acts against the law, "is only the unreal shadow," for "he [sic] exists merely as a universal self" (282). In other words, anyone who commits the deed that he does will be guilty; the individual, through crime, loses his individuality and becomes such an "anyone." Then, without advance warning, Hegel appears to introduce Antigone without naming her: he remarks that the one who commits a crime according to prevailing universal standards of *Sittlichkeit* is caught in the position of breaking human law in following divine law, and breaking divine law in following human law: "The deed has only carried out one law in contrast to the other" (283). Thus the one who acts according to the law, where the law is always *either* human *or* divine but *not both*, is always blind to the law that is disobeyed at that instant. This leads him to the figure of Oedipus through the following route: "Actuality therefore holds concealed within it the other aspect which is alien to this knowledge [the resolve that knows what it does], and does not reveal the whole truth about itself to consciousness [Die Wirklichkeit hält daher die andere dem Wissen fremde Seite in sich verborgen, und zeigt sich dem Bewusstsein nicht, wie sie an und für sich ist]: the son does not recognize his father in the man who has wronged him and whom he slays, nor his mother in the queen whom he makes his wife" (283, 347).

Thus, Hegel explains that guilt becomes explicitly experienced in the doing of the deed, in the experience of the "breaking through" of one law *in and through* another, "seiz[ing] the doer in the act [Dem sittlichen Selbstbewusstsein stellt auf diese Weise eine lichtscheue Macht nach, welche erst, *wenn die tat geschehen, hervorbricht und es bei ihr ergreift*]" (283, 347, my emphasis). Still in reference to Oedipus, then, Hegel writes: "The doer cannot deny the crime or his guilt: the significance of the deed is that what was unmoved has been set in motion" and, in his word, "the unconscious" has been "linked together with the conscious [und hiermit das Unbewusste dem Bewussten, das Nichtseiende dem Sein zu verknüpfen]" (283, 347, my translation). This leads Hegel to talk about a "right" that is tacitly asserted in the commission of crime, a right that is not yet known except in and through the awareness of guilt.

Hegel underscores the link between guilt and entitlement, a claim to entitlement that is implicit in guilt, an entitlement, an access to a right that is necessarily and at the same time an abrogation of another law. Here he seems to be referring to Oedipus who unknowingly commits his crimes and is overcome with guilt in retrospect. Antigone does not appear to feel guilt, though she does assert her right, even as she acknowledges that the "law" that justifies her act is one that Creon can regard only as a sign of criminality. For Hegel, the unconscious, or what he describes as "nonexisting," emerges in the claim of entitlement, the act that grounds itself in a law that counts as no law within the realm of law. There is no justification for the claim Antigone makes. The law she invokes is one that has only one possible instance of application and is not, within any ordinary sense, conceptualizable as law. What is this law beyond law, beyond conceptualization, which makes her act and her defense in speech appear as nothing other than a breaking of law, a law that emerges as the breaking of law? Is this one kind of law that offers grounds for breaking another kind of law, and can these grounds be enumerated, conceptualized, and transposed from context to context? Or is this a law that defies conceptualization and that stands as an epistemic scandal within the realm of law, a law that cannot be translated, that marks the very limit of legal conceptualization, a breakage in law performed, as it were, by a legality that remains uncontained by any and all positive and generalizable law? This is a legality of what does not exist and of what is unconscious, not a law *of* the unconscious but some form of demand that the unconscious necessarily makes on law, that which marks the limit and condition of law's generalizability.[4]

Hegel points to this moment, almost founders upon it, but is quick to contain its scandalous consequence. He distinguishes Oedipus from Antigone, establishing the excusability of his crime, the inexcusability of hers. He does this precisely by ridding her action of any unconscious motivation, and identifying her with a fully conscious act: "The ethical consciousness is more complete, its guilt more inexcusable, if it knows *beforehand* the law and the power which it opposes, if it takes them to be violence and wrong, to be ethical merely by accident, and, like Antigone, knowingly commits the crime [wissentlich . . . das Verbrechen begeht]." As if taking on the point of view of Creon who cannot get Antigone to perform a full enough confession for him, Hegel concludes this discussion with the claim that "The ethical consciousness must, on account of this actuality and on account of its deed, acknowledge its opposite as its own actuality, [and] must acknowledge its guilt" (284, 348). The opposite of her action is the law that she defies, and Hegel bids Antigone to acknowledge the legitimacy of that law.

Antigone, of course, acknowledges her deed, but the verbal form of her acknowledgment only exacerbates the crime. She not only did it, but she had the nerve to *say* she did it. Thus Antigone cannot exemplify the ethical consciousness who suffers guilt; she is beyond guilt—she embraces her crime as she embraces her death, her tomb, her bridal chamber. At this point in his text, Hegel cites Antigone herself, as if her words support his point: "weil wir leiden, anerkennen wir, dass wir gefehlt,"[5] translated by Miller as "because we suffer we acknowledge we have erred" (284, 348). But consider the qualification of this remark that enters with Grene's translation: "If this proceeding is good in the gods' eyes/I shall know my sin, once I have suffered" (982–983).[6] And note the extraordinary suspension of the question of guilt and the implicit rebuke to Hegel that enters with the most reliable translation, that offered by Lloyd-Jones: "Well, if this is approved among the gods, I should forgive [syggignosko] them for what I have suffered, since I have done wrong; but if they are the wrongdoers, may they not suffer worse evils than those they are unjustly inflicting upon me!"

Here Antigone seems to know and to speak the wisdom that she cannot quite avow, for Antigone will not admit her guilt. This appears to be the first reason that Hegel gives for why she does not gain admission into the ethical law.[7] Antigone does not deny that she has done the deed, but this does not qualify as an admission of guilt for Hegel. Indeed, to admit guilt as Hegel and Creon would have her do would be to exercise public speech in precisely the way she is not permitted to do. One wonders whether women could ever suffer guilt in Hegel's sense, for the self-consciousness of the guilty and repentant person is of necessity mediated by the sphere of the state. In fact, to exercise that speech, in precisely the way that she does, is to commit a different kind of offense, the one in which a prepolitical subject lays claim to a rageful agency within the public sphere. The public sphere, as I am calling it here, is called variably the community, government, and the state by Hegel; it only acquires its existence through *interfering* with the happiness of the family; thus, it creates for itself "an internal enemy—womankind in general. Womankind—the everlasting irony [in the life] of the community" (288, 352).

The introduction of womankind seems clearly to draw on the prior reference to Antigone, but it also, curiously, supplants that reference, in much the same way that Hegel alters her language to suit his ethical format. At first it appears that Hegel's claims about Antigone might well apply to the "*Weiblichkeit*" at hand:

> Womankind . . . changes by intrigue the universal end of the government into a private end, transforms its universal activity [allgemeine Tätigkeit] into a work of some particular individual, and perverts the universal property [verkehrt das allgemeine Eigentum] of the state into a possession and ornament for the Family [zu einem Besitz und Putz der Familie].
>
> *(288, 353)*

This sudden shift to the subject of womankind recalls Antigone but also clearly generalizes from her case in a way that effaces her name and her particularity. This "womankind" perverts the universal, making the state into possessions and ornaments for the family, decorating the family with the paraphernalia of the state, making banners and shawls out of the state apparatus. This perversion of universality has no political implications. Indeed, "womankind" does not act politically but constitutes a perversion and privatization of the political sphere, a sphere governed by universality.

Although earlier Hegel implies that Antigone's perversion of universality, despite its appearance of criminality, may actually be the eruption of a legality from another order, one that can only appear as criminality from the point of view of universality, he sees no such unconscious eruption of entitlement in the perversion of universality that women generally perform. Indeed, at the very moment in Hegel's text where Antigone becomes *generalized* as femininity or womankind, the perversion in question loses its scandalous place in the political field, devaluing the political as private property and ornamentality. In other words, by supplanting Antigone with "womankind," Hegel performs the very generalization that Antigone resists, a generalization according to which Antigone can only be held criminal and that, consequentially, effaces her from Hegel's text.

The feminine figure who takes the place of Antigone and bears the residual trace of her crime thus ridicules the universal, transposes its operation, and devalues its meaning through the overvaluation of male youth, thus recalling Antigone's love for Polyneices.[8] This love cannot remain within the sphere of kinship, however, and must lead instead to its own sacrifice, a sacrifice of the son to the state for the purposes of waging war. It is not the incest taboo that interrupts the love that family members have for one another; rather, it is the action of the state engaged in war. The effort to pervert by feminine means the universality for which the state stands is thus crushed by a countermovement of the state, one that not only interferes with the happiness of the family but enlists the family in the service of its own militarization. The state receives its army from the family, and the family meets its dissolution in the state.

To the extent that we are now talking of a mother who sacrifices her son for war, we are no longer talking about Antigone. For Antigone is no mother and has no son. As one who appears to put family first, she is guilty of a crime against the state and, more particularly, of a criminal individualism. Acting thus in the name of the state, Hegel's writing moves to suppress Antigone and to offer a rationale for this suppression: "The community . . . can only maintain itself by suppressing this spirit of individualism."[9]

From this discussion of the hostility toward the individual and toward womankind as a representative of individuality, Hegel moves to a discussion of war, that is, a form of hostility necessary for the community's self-definition.[10] The woman earlier described as finding promise of pleasure and dignity in the male youth now finds that the youth enters war and that she is under a state obligation to send him. The community's necessary aggression against womankind (its internal enemy) appears to be transmuted into the community's aggression against its external enemy; the state intervenes in the family to wage war. The worth of the warring male youth is openly acknowledged, and in this way the community now loves him as she has loved him. This investment is taken over by the community as it applauds the sons who have gone to war, an investment that is understood to preserve and consolidate the state. If, earlier, she "perverted" the universal property of the state as "possession and property of the family," the state now reclaims the love of male youth, reestablishing itself as the source of all valuation and recognition. The state now substitutes itself for womankind, and that figure of woman is at once absorbed and jettisoned, presumed as the state's necessary presumption at the same time it is repudiated as part of its proper field of operation. Thus Hegel's text transmutes Antigone in such a way that her criminality loses the force of the alternative legality that it carries, after which she is translated once again into a maternal womankind that she never becomes. Finally, that doubly displaced figure is itself repudiated by a state apparatus that absorbs and repudiates her desire. Whoever she is, she is, quite obviously, left behind, left behind for war, left behind for the homosociality of state desire. Indeed, this is the last mention of her name in the text, a name that represented the conflict of one law by and through another that now, erased, is less resolved than cast aside. The universality of the ethical order does not contain her but only the trace of her doubly expropriated love.

Hegel returns to Antigone in *The Philosophy of Right* where he makes clear that she is associated with a set of laws that are finally not compatible with public law.[11] "This law," he writes, "is there displayed as a law opposed to public law, to the law of the land."[12] Hegel also writes: "If we consider ethical life from the objective standpoint, we may say that we are ethical unselfconsciously" (259). Here Antigone is invested with an unconscious, when she affirms in the following passage the irrecoverability of the origins of law: "No one knows whence the laws come; they are everlasting" is the line (455) that Hegel cites. In the Lloyd-Jones translation, the line is augmented to emphasize the vital animation of the law; Antigone speaks to Creon: "Nor did I think your proclamations strong enough to have power to overrule, mortal as they were, the unwritten and unfailing ordinances of the gods. For these have life, not simply today and yesterday, but forever, and no one knows how long ago they were revealed" (450–456).

Hegel has clearly identified the law for which Antigone speaks as the unwritten law of the ancient gods, one that appears only by way of an active trace. Indeed, what kind of law would it be? A law for which no origin can be found, a law whose trace can take no form, whose authority is not directly communicable through written language. If it is communicable, this law would emerge through speech, but a speech that cannot be spoken from script and, so, certainly not the speech of a play, unless the play calls upon a legality, as it were, prior to its own scene of enunciation, unless the play commits a crime against this legality precisely by speaking it. Thus the figure of this other law calls into question the literalism of the play, *Antigone*: no words in this play will give us this law, no words in this play will recite the strictures of this law. How, then, will it be discerned?

This law, we are told, is in opposition to public law; as the unconscious of public law, it is that which public law cannot do without, which it must, in fact, oppose and retain with a certain necessary hostility. Thus Hegel cites Antigone's word, a citation that contains and expels her at once, in which she refers to the unwritten and unfailing status of these laws. The laws of which she speaks are, strictly speaking, before writing, not yet registered or registerable at the level of writing. They are not fully knowable, but the state knows enough about them to oppose them violently. Although these laws are unwritten, she nevertheless speaks in their name, and so they emerge only in the form of catachresis that serves as the prior condition and limit to written codification. They are not radically autonomous, for they are already taken up by the written and public law as that which must be contained, subordinated, and opposed. And yet, this will be nearly impossible, if only because the catachrestic reference to the unwritten and unwritable law in the form of dramatic speech and, indeed, in the Sophoclean script attest to this non-codifiable and excessive condition of public law. The public law, however, as much as it opposes the nonpublic or nonpublishable condition of its own emergence, reproduces the very excess it seeks to contain.

Hegel attends to Antigone's act, but not to her speech, perhaps because that speech would be impossible were she to represent the unrepresentable law. If what she represents is precisely what remains unconscious within public law, then she exists for Hegel at the limit of the publicly knowable and codifiable. Although this is sometimes marked by Hegel as precisely *another* law, it is also acknowledged as a law that leaves only an incommunicable trace, an enigma of another possible order. If she "is" anything, she is the unconscious of the law, that which is presupposed by public reality but that cannot appear within its terms.

Hegel not only accepts her fatal disappearance from the public stage but helps to usher her off that stage and into her living tomb. He does not, for instance, account for how it is that she *does* appear, through what misappropriation of the public discourse her act becomes recognized as a public act. Does the unwritten law have the power to rewrite public law; is it the not yet written, or is it the never to be written that constitutes an invariable incommensurability between the two spheres?

Just as what appears criminal from the sovereign perspective of Creon and, indeed, from the universal perspective of Hegel can contain within it an unconscious demand, one that marks the limits of both sovereign and universal authority, so one might reapproach Antigone's "fatality" with the question of whether the limit for which she stands, a limit for which no standing, no translatable representation is possible, is not precisely the trace of an alternate legality that haunts the conscious, public sphere as its scandalous future.

One might expect that the turn to Lacan would usher in a more nuanced and promising consideration of the unconscious, but I would like to suggest that his reading also relocates Antigone's fatality in terms of the necessary limits of kinship. The law that mandates her unlivability is not one that might profitably be broken. And if Hegel comes to stand for the law of the state, Lacan deploys Antigone's apparent perversion to confirm an intractable law of kinship.

Lacan will take radical distance from Hegel, objecting to the opposition between human and divine law, concentrating instead on the internal conflict of a desire that can meet its limit only in death. Antigone, he writes, is at "the threshold" of the symbolic, but how are we to understand a threshold? It is not a transition, superseded and retained in the forward motion of Spirit. At once the outside, the entry, the limit without which the symbolic cannot be thought, it remains, nevertheless, unthinkable within the symbolic. At the threshold of the symbolic, Antigone appears as a figure who inaugurates its operation. But where precisely is this threshold and entry? The unwritten and unfailing laws to which Antigone refers, and that Hegel identifies as the law of the feminine, are *not* the same as the symbolic domain, and the symbolic is not quite the same as public law. Are these laws with no clear origin and of uncertain authorization something like a symbolic order, an alternative symbolic or imaginary in the Irigarayan sense, one that constitutes the unconscious of public law, the unknowing feminine condition of its possibility?

Before I consider Lacan's answer to this question, I would like to take a moment to reconsider his version of the symbolic order and perhaps offer a set of revisions to the brief account I offered in the last chapter.

In Lacan's second seminar, he offers under the title of "The Symbolic Universe" a conversation with Jean Hyppolite and Octave Mannoni on the work of Lévi-Strauss, on the distinction between nature and symbol. Lacan clarifies the importance of the symbolic in the work of Lévi-Strauss and thereby clarifies his own indebtedness to Lévi-Strauss for the theorization of the symbolic order. The conversation begins with Lacan rehearsing Lévi-Strauss's point of view: kinship and the family cannot be derived from any naturalistic cause, and even the incest taboo is not biologically motivated.[13] From where, then, he asks, do the elementary structures of kinship emerge? At the close of *The Elementary Structures of Kinship*, the exchange of women is considered as the trafficking of a sign, the linguistic currency that facilitates a symbolic and communicative bond among men. The exchange of women is likened to the exchange of words, and this particular linguistic circuitry becomes the basis for rethinking kinship on the basis of linguistic structures, the totality of which is called the symbolic. Within that structuralist understanding of the symbolic, every sign invokes the totality of the symbolic order in which it functions. Kinship ceases to be thought in terms of blood relations or naturalized social arrangements but becomes the effect of a linguistic set of relations in which each term signifies only and always in relation to other terms.

Taking this moment to be salient, Lacan emphasizes that kinship appears no longer as a function of a naturalistic biology: "In the human order, we are dealing with the complete emergence of a new function, encompassing the whole order in its entirety

[à l'émergence totale englobant tout l'ordre humain dans sa total-
ité—d'une fonction nouvelle]" (29, 42). Although Lévi-Strauss's
theorization of the symbolic is new, the symbolic function is
always already there or, rather, has precisely such an effect, to
establish itself *sub specie aeternitatis*. Indeed, Lacan writes of the
symbolic in ways that suggest a convergence with Antigone's
unwritten law whose origins are similarly inhuman and indis-
cernible: "The symbolic function is not new as a function, it has
its beginnings elsewhere [amorces ailleurs] than in the human
order, but they are only beginnings [il ne s'agit que d'amorces].
The human order is characterized by the fact that the symbolic
function intervenes at every moment and at every stage [le
degrés] of its existence" (29, 42).

Like Antigone's unwritten laws, the ones that, according to
Hegel, appear as divine and subjective, governing the feminine
structure of the family, these laws are not codifiable but are understood fundamentally as "tied to a circular process of the exchange
of speech." "There is," Lacan writes in a later portion of the seminar, "a symbolic circuit external to the subject, tied to a certain
group of supports, of human agents, in which the subject, the
small circle which is called his destiny, is indeterminately included"
(98).[14] These signs travel their circuitry, are spoken by subjects,
but are not originated by the subjects who speak them. They
arrive, as it were, as the "discourse of the other [which] is the discourse of the circuit in which I am integrated" (89). Lacan remarks
of the symbolic in the essay "The Circuit": "I am one of its links
[un des chaînons]. It is the discourse of my father, for instance, in
so far as my father made mistakes which I am absolutely condemned to reproduce—that's what we call *the super-ego*" (89, 112).

Thus the circuitry of the symbolic is identified with the father's
word echoing in the subject, dividing its temporality between an
irrecoverable elsewhere and the time of its present utterance.
Lacan understands this symbolic bequest as a demand and an
obligation: "It is precisely my duty to transmit [the chain of dis-

course] in aberrant form to someone else [Je suis justement chargé de la transmettre dans sa forme aberrante à quelqu'un d'autre]" (89, 112).

Significantly, the subject is not identifiable with the symbolic, for the symbolic circuitry is always to some extent external to the subject. And yet there is no escape from the symbolic. This prompts Hyppolite to complain directly to Lacan: "The symbolic function is for you, if I understand it correctly, a transcendental function [une fonction de transcendance], in the sense that, quite simultaneously, we can neither remain in it, nor can we get out of it. What purpose does it serve? We cannot do without it, and yet we cannot inhabit it either" (38, 51). Lacan's reply is to affirm what he has already said and so to display the repetitive function of the law: "If the symbolic function functions, we are inside it. And I would even say—we are so far into it that we can't get out of it. [Je dirai plus—nous sommes tellement à l'intérieur que nous ne pouvons en sortir]" (31, 43).

And yet it will not be right to say that we are either fully "in" or "outside" this symbolic law: for Lacan, "the symbolic order is what is most elevated in man and what isn't in man, but elsewhere" (116). As a permanent elsewhere that is "in" man, the symbolic decenters the subject that it engenders. But what is the status of this elsewhere? An elsewhere to the human order, the symbolic is not, therefore, precisely divine. But let us consider as a qualification to this last disavowal Lévi-Strauss's own fear, reported by Lacan, that he might be ushering God out one door only to usher God in through another. Lacan emphasizes instead that the symbolic is universal and contingent at once, enforcing an appearance of its universality but having no mandate outside itself that might serve as a transcendental ground for its own functioning. Its function is to transcendentalize its claims, but this is not the same as saying that it has or maintains a transcendental ground. The effect of transcendentality is an effect of the claim itself.

Lacan writes, "This order constitutes a totality . . . [t]he symbolic order from the first takes on its universal character." And later: "As soon as the symbol arrives, there is a universe of symbols" (29). This is not to say that the symbolic is universal in the sense of being universally valid for all time, but only that, every time it appears, it appears as a universalizing function; it refers to the chain of signs through which it derives its own signifying power. Lacan remarks that symbolic agencies crosscut differences among societies as the structure of an unconscious radically irreducible to social life.[15] Similarly, Lacan will say that the Oedipus complex, a structure of the symbolic, is both universal and contingent precisely "because it is uniquely and purely symbolic": it represents what cannot be, strictly speaking, what has been alleviated from being in its status as a linguistic substitution for the ontologically given. It does not capture or display its object. This furtive and missing object nevertheless only becomes intelligible by appearing, displaced, within the substitutions that constitute symbolic terms. The symbolic might be understood as a certain kind of tomb that does not precisely extinguish that which nevertheless remains living and trapped within its terms, a site where Antigone, already half-dead within the intelligible, is bound not to survive. On this reading, the symbolic thus captures Antigone, and though she commits suicide in that tomb, there remains a question of whether or not she might signify in a way that exceeds the reach of the symbolic.

Although Lacan's theorization of the symbolic is meant to take the place of those accounts of kinship grounded in nature or theology, it continues to wield the force of universality. Its "contingency" describes the way in which it remains incommensurable with any subject who inhabits its terms, and the lack of any final transcendental ground for its operation. In no way, however, is the universalizing effect of its own operation called into question by the assertion of contingency here. Thus structures of kinship cast as symbolic continue to produce a universalizing effect.

How, under these conditions, does the very effect of universality become rendered as contingent, much less undermined, rewritten, and subject to transformation?

For the Oedipus complex to be universal by virtue of being symbolic, for Lacan, does *not* mean that the Oedipus complex has to be globally evidenced for it to be regarded as universal. The problem is not that the symbolic represents a false universal. Rather, where and when the Oedipus complex appears, it exercises the function of universalization: it *appears* as that which is everywhere true. In this sense, it is not a universal concretely realized or realizable; its failure at realization is precisely what sustains its status as a universal possibility. No exception can call this universality into question precisely because it does not rely on empirical instantiation to support its universalizing function (that function is radically unsupported and, hence, contingent in that restricted sense). Indeed, its particularization would be its ruination.

But does this understanding of universalization work to usher in God (or the gods) through another door? If the Oedipus complex is not universal in one way, but remains universal in another, does it finally matter which way it is universal if the effect is the same? Note that the sense in which the incest taboo is "contingent" is precisely that of "ungrounded"; but what follows from this ungroundedness? It does not follow that the taboo itself might appear as radically alterable or, indeed, eliminable; rather, to the extent that it does appear, it appears in a universal form. Thus this contingency, an ungroundedness that becomes the condition of a universalizing appearance, is radically distinct from a contingency that establishes the variability and limited cultural operation of any such rule or norm.

Lacan's approach to Antigone takes place within the question of ethics in *Seminar VII*.[16] He has been discussing the problem of the good, as a category central to ethics and commodification. "How is it that at the moment that everything is organized around the power to do good, something completely enigmatic proposes itself to us and returns to us ceaselessly from our own action as its unknown consequence?" (F, 275, my translation). Hegel, he writes, "is nowhere weaker than he is in the sphere of poetics, and this is especially true of what he has to say about *Antigone*" (E, 249). He makes a mistake in the *Phenomenology* to claim that *Antigone* reveals a "clear opposition . . . between the discourse of the family and that of the state. But in my opinion things are much less clear" (236).

Championing Goethe's reading, Lacan insists that "Creon is [not] opposed to Antigone as one principle of the law, of discourse, to another. . . . Goethe shows that Creon is driven by his desire and manifestly deviates from the straight path . . . he rushes by himself to his own destruction [il court à sa perte]" (254, 297).

In a sense, Lacan's concern with the play is precisely with this rushing by oneself to one's own destruction, that fatal rushing that structures the action of Creon and Antigone alike. Thus Lacan resituates the problematic of *Antigone* as an internal difficulty of "the desire to do good," the desire to live in conformity with an ethical norm. Something invariably emerges in the very trajectory of desire that appears enigmatic or mysterious from the conscious point of view that is oriented toward the pursuit of the good: "In the irreducible margin as well as at the limit of his own good, the subject reveals himself to the never entirely resolved mystery of the nature of his desire [le sujet se révèle au mystère irrésolu de ce qu'est son désir]" (237, 278). Lacan refers Antigone to the notion of the beautiful, suggesting that the beautiful is not always compatible with the desire for the good, suggesting as well that it lures and fascinates us because of its enigmatic character. Antigone will emerge, then, for Lacan as a problem of beauty, fascination, and death as precisely what intervenes between the desire for the good, the desire to conform to the ethical norm, and thereby derails it, enigmatically, from its path. This is, then, not an opposition between one discourse or principle and another, between the family and the community, but a conflict internal to and constitutive of the operation of desire and, in particular, ethical desire.

Lacan objects to Hegel's insistence that the play moves toward a "reconciliation" of two principles (249). Hegel thus reads the death drive out of desire. Lacan repeatedly makes the case that "it isn't simply the defense of the sacred rights of the dead and of the family," but it *is* about the trajectory of passion that winds its way toward self-destruction. But here he suggests that the thinking of fatal passion is finally separable from the constraints imposed by kinship. Is this separation possible, considering the specter of incestuous passion, and is any theorization of the symbolic or its inauguration finally separable from the question of kinship and the family? After all, we saw in *Seminar II* how the very notion of the symbolic is derived from his reading of Lévi-Strauss on the elementary structures of kinship and, in particular, on the figure of woman as a linguistic object of exchange. Indeed, Lacan reports that he has asked Lévi-Strauss to reread Antigone in order to confirm that the play is about the inception of culture itself (285).

Nevertheless, Antigone is approached by Lacan first as a fascinating image and then in relation to the problem of the death drive in masochism. In relation to this last, however, Lacan suggests that the unwritten and unfailing laws prior to all codification are those that mark the far side of a symbolic limit beyond which humans may not cross. Antigone appears at this limit or, indeed, as this limit, and most of Lacan's subsequent discussion focuses on the term *Atè*, understood as the limit of human existence that can be crossed only briefly within life.

Antigone is already in the service of death, dead while living, and so she appears to have crossed over in some way to a death that remains to be understood. Lacan takes her obstinacy to be a manifestation of this death drive, joining with the chorus in calling her "inhuman" (263) in relation to Ismene, and she is clearly not the only one to be "of" this prior and unwritten realm: Creon wants to promote the good of all as the law without limits (259), but in the process of applying the law, exceeds the law, basing his authority as well in unwritten laws that seem to propel his own actions toward self-destruction. Teiresias as well is understood to speak precisely from this place that is not exactly "of" life: his voice is and is not his own, his words come from the gods, from the boy who describes the signs, from the words he receives from others, and yet he is the one who speaks. His authority also appears to come from some other place than the human. His speaking of the divine words establishes him as one for whom mimesis entails a splitting and a loss of autonomy; it links him to the kind of speaking that Creon performs in asserting his authority beyond its codifiable bounds. Not only does his speech come from a place other than human life, it also portends or produces—or, rather, relays a return to—another death, the second death that Lacan identifies as the cessation of all transformations, natural or historical.

Lacan clearly links Antigone to Sacher-Masoch and to Sade in this portion of the seminar: "Analysis shows clearly that the subject separates out a double of himself who is made inaccessible to destruction, so as to make it support what, borrowing a term from the realm of aesthetics, one cannot help calling the play of pain." Torture establishes indestructibility for both Antigone and Sade. The indestructible support becomes the occasion for the production of forms, and so the condition of aesthetics itself. In Lacan's terms, "The object [in the sadean fantasm] is no more than the power to support a form of suffering" (261) and thus becomes a form of persistence that survives efforts at its destruction. This persistence appears linked with what Lacan, in Spinozistic fashion, calls pure Being.

Lacan's discussion of Antigone in *Seminar VII* unfolds in metonymic ways, identifying at first the way in which the play forces a revision of Aristotle's theory of catharsis. Lacan suggests that *Antigone* does involve purgation—or expiation—but that it is not one that leads to the restoration of calm but rather to the continuation of irresolution. He asks more specifically about the "image" of Antigone (248) in relation to this purgation without resolve and defines it as an image that purifies everything pertaining to the order of the imaginary (248). This same pivotal feature of Antigone leads metonymically to a consideration of "the second death," one that Lacan describes as nullifying the conditions of the first death, namely, the cycle of death and life. The second death is thus one for which there is no redemptive cycle, for which no birth follows: this will be Antigone's death but, according to her soliloquy, it will have been the death of every member of her family. Lacan further identifies this second death with "Being itself," borrowing the convention of capitalization from the Heideggerian lexicon. The image of Antigone, the image of irresolution, the irresolved image, is the position of Being itself.

Earlier on this same page, however, Lacan links this same image to "tragic action," one that he later claims articulates the position of Being as a limit. Significantly, this limit is also described in terms of a constitutive irresolution, namely, "being buried alive in a tomb." Later, he gives us other language with which to understand this irresolved image, that of motionless moving (252). This image is also said to "fascinate" and to exercise an effect on desire—an image that will turn out, at the end of "The Splendor of Antigone," to be constitutive of desire itself. In the theater we watch those who are buried alive in a tomb, we watch the dead move, we watch with fascination as the inanimate is animated.

It seems that the irresolvable coincidence of life and death in the image, the image that Antigone exemplifies without exhausting, is also what is meant by the "limit" and the "position of Being." This is a limit that is not precisely thinkable within life but that acts in life as the boundary over which the living cannot cross, a limit that constitutes and negates life simultaneously.

When Lacan claims that Antigone fascinates as an image, and that she is "beautiful" (260), he is calling attention to this simultaneous and irresolvable coincidence of life and death that she brings into relief for her audience. She is dying, but alive, and so signifies the limit that (final) death is. Lacan turns to Sade in this discussion in order to make clear that the null point, the "start[ing] again from zero," is what occasions the production and reproduction of forms; it is "a substratum that makes suffering bearable . . . the double of oneself" that provides the support for pain (261). Again, on the next page, Lacan makes this clear by delineating the conditions of endurance, describing the constitutive feature of this image as "the limit in which a being remains in a state of suffering" (262).

Thus, Lacan attempts to show that Antigone cannot finally be understood in light of the historical legacies from which she emerges but, rather, as asserting "a right that emerges in the ineffaceable character of what is" (279). And this leads him to the controversial conclusion that "that separation of being from the characteristics of the historical drama he has lived through, is precisely the limit or the *ex nihilo* to which Antigone is attached" (279). Here, again, one might well ask how the historical drama she has lived through returns her not only to this persistent ineffaceability of what is but the certain prospect of effaceability. By separating the historical drama she lives through from the metaphysical truth she exemplifies for us, Lacan fails to ask how certain kinds of lives, precisely by virtue of the historical drama that is theirs, are relegated to the limits of the ineffaceable.

Like other Sophoclean characters, those in *Antigone* are for Lacan, "at a limit that is not accounted for by their solitude relative to others" (272). They are not just separated from one another or, indeed, separated from one another through reference to the singularizing effect of finitude. There is something more: they are characters who find themselves "right away in a limit zone, find themselves between life and death" (272), conveyed by Lacan as one hyphenated word: "*entre-la-vie-et-la-mort*" (F, 317). Unlike Hegel, Lacan understands that the mandate under which

Antigone acts is importantly ambiguous, producing a claim whose status is not in any clear opposition to Creon's. She is, first of all, appealing to *both* the laws of the earth and the commandments of the gods (276), and her discourse, accordingly, vacillates between them. She attempts to distinguish herself from Creon, but are their desires so very different from one another? Similarly, the chorus seeks to dissociate itself from what Lacan calls "the desire of the other" but finds that this separation is finally impossible. Both Creon and Antigone at different moments claim that the gods are on their side: Creon grounds the laws of the city with reference to the decrees of the gods; Antigone cites the chthonic gods as her authority. Do they appeal to the same gods, and what kind of gods are they and what havoc have they wrought, if both Antigone and Creon understand themselves to be within the circuitry of their mandate?

For Lacan, to seek recourse to the gods is precisely to seek recourse beyond human life, to seek recourse to death and to instate that death within life; this recourse to what is beyond or before the symbolic leads to a self-destruction that literalizes the importation of death into life. It is as if the very invocation of that elsewhere precipitates desire in the direction of death, a second death, one that signifies the foreclosure of any further transformation. Antigone, in particular, "violates the limits of *Atè* through her desire" (277). If this is a limit that humans can cross only briefly or, more aptly, cannot cross for long,[17] it is one she has not only crossed but beyond which she has remained far too long. She has crossed the line, defying public law, citing a law from elsewhere, but this elsewhere is a death that is also solicited by that very citation. She acts, but acts according to a command of death, one that returns to her by destroying the continuing condition of possibility for her very act, her finally insupportable act.

Lacan writes: "The limit in question is one on which she establishes herself, a place where she feels herself to be unassailable, a place where it is impossible for a mortal being to go beyond the laws. *These are no longer laws but a certain legality which is a conse-quence of the laws of the gods that are said to be . . . unwritten . . . an invocation of something that is, in effect, of the order of law, but which is not developed in any signifying chain or in anything else* [dans rien]" (278, 324, my emphasis). Thus she does not establish her-self within the symbolic, and these unwritten and unwritable laws are not the same as the symbolic, that circuitry of exchange within which the subject finds herself. Although Lacan identifies this death-driven movement internal to desire as what finally takes her out of the symbolic, that condition for a supportable life, it is peculiar that what moves her across the barrier to the scene of death is precisely the curse of her father, the father's words, the very terms by which Lacan earlier *defines* the symbolic: "The dis-course of my father, for instance, in so far as my father made mis-takes which I am absolutely condemned to reproduce—that's what we call the *super-ego*." If the demand or duty imposed by the symbolic is "to transmit the chain of discourse in aberrant form to someone else" (*Seminar II*, 89), then Antigone transmits that chain but also, significantly, by obeying the curse upon her, stops the future operation of that chain.

Although she operates within the terms of the law when she makes her claim for justice, she also destroys the basis of justice in community by insisting that her brother is irreducible to any law that would render citizens interchangeable with one another. As she asserts his radical particularity, he comes to stand as a scandal, as the threat of ruination to the universality of law.

In a sense, Antigone refuses to allow her love for her brother to become assimilated to a symbolic order that requires the com-municability of the sign. By remaining on the side of the incom-municable sign, the unwritten law, she refuses to submit her love to the chain of signification, that life of substitutability that lan-guage inaugurates. She stands, Lacan tells us, for "the ineffaceable character of what is" (279). But what *is*, under the rule of the sym-bolic, is precisely what is evacuated through the emergence of the sign. The return to an ineffaceable ontology, prelinguistic, is thus associated in Lacan with a return to death and, indeed, with a death drive (referentiality here figured as death).

But consider that, *pace* Lacan, Antigone, in standing for Polyneices, and for her love of Polyneices, does not simply stand for the ineffaceable character of what is. First of all, it is the exposed body of her brother that she seeks to cover, if not to efface, by her burial of dust. Second, it seems that one reason that standing for her brother implicates her in a death in life is that it abrogates precisely the kinship relations that articulate the Lacanian symbolic, the intelligible conditions for life. She does not merely enter death by leaving the symbolic bonds of community to retrieve an impossible and pure ontology of the brother. What Lacan elides at this moment, manifesting his own blindness perhaps, is that she suffers a fatal condemnation by virtue of abrogating the incest taboo that articulates kinship and the symbolic. It is not that the pure content of the brother is irretrievable from behind the symbolic articulation of the brother but that the symbolic itself is limited by its constitutive interdictions.

Lacan casts the problem in terms of an inverse relation between the symbolic and a pure ontology: "Antigone's position represents the radical limit that affirms the unique value of his being without reference to any content, to whatever good or evil Polyneices may have done, or to whatever he may be subjected to."[18] But this analysis forgets that she is also committing a crime, not only defying the edict of the state but the crime of carrying her love for her brother too far. Who, then, separates Polyneices from "the historical drama he has lived through" but Lacan himself, generalizing the fatal effects of this interdiction as " the break that the very presence of language inaugurates in the life of man."

It seems here that what is forgotten, buried, or covered over is precisely Lacan's earlier linking of the symbolic to Lévi-Strauss and the question of whether or not that symbolic is a "totality" as Lévi-Strauss claimed and as Hyppolite feared. If, as Lacan claims,

Antigone represents a kind of thinking that counters the symbolic and, hence, counters life, perhaps it is precisely because the very terms of livability are established by a symbolic that is challenged by her kind of claim. And this claim does not take place outside the symbolic or, indeed, outside the public sphere, but within its terms and as an unanticipated appropriation and perversion of its own mandate.

The curse of the father is in fact how Lacan defines the symbolic, that obligation of the progeny to carry on in their own aberrant directions his very words. The words of the father, the inaugurating utterances of the symbolic curse connect his children in one stroke. These words become the circuit within which her desire takes form, and though she is entangled in these words, even hopelessly, they do not quite capture her. Do these words not condemn her to death, since Oedipus claims that it would have been better had his children not lived, or is it her escape from those words that lead her into the unlivability of a desire outside cultural intelligibility? If the symbolic is governed by the words of the father, and the symbolic is structured by a kinship that has assumed the form of linguistic structure, and Antigone's desire is insupportable within the symbolic, then why does Lacan maintain that it is some immanent feature of her desire that leads her inexorably toward death? Is it not precisely the limits of kinship that are registered as the insupportability of desire, which turns desire toward death?

Lacan acknowledges that there is a limit here, but this will be the limit of culture itself, a necessary limit beyond which death is necessary. He asserts that "life can only be approached, can only be lived or thought about, from the place of that limit where her life is already lost, where she is already on the other side" (280). But to what extent can this death-driven thought return to challenge the articulation of the symbolic and to alter the fatal interdictions by which it reproduces its own field of power? And what of her fate is in fact a social death, in the sense that Orlando Patterson has used that term?[19] This seems a crucial question, for this position outside life as we know it is not necessarily a position outside life as it must be. It provides a perspective on the symbolic constraints under which livability is established, and the question becomes: Does it also provide a critical perspective by which the very terms of livability might be rewritten, or indeed, written for the first time.

Does she, as Lacan suggests, "push to the limit the realization of something that might be called the pure and simple desire of death as such" (282)? And is her desire merely to persist in criminality to the point of death? Is Lacan right that "Antigone chooses to be purely and simply the guardian of the being of the criminal as such" (283), or does this criminality assert an unconscious right, marking a legality prior to codification on which the symbolic in its hasty foreclosures must founder, establishing the question of whether there might be new grounds for communicability and for life?

CHAPTER 3
Promiscuous Obedience

In George Steiner's study of the historical appropriations of *Antigone*, he poses a controversial question he does not pursue: What would happen if psychoanalysis were to have taken Antigone rather than Oedipus as its point of departure?[1] Oedipus clearly has his own tragic fate, but Antigone's fate is decidedly postoedipal. Although her brothers are explicitly cursed by her father, does the curse also work on her and, if so, through what furtive and implicit means? The chorus remarks that something of Oedipus' fate is surely working through her own, but what burden of history does she bear? Oedipus comes to know who his mother and father are but finds that his mother is also his wife. Antigone's father is her brother, since they both share a mother in Jocasta, and her brothers are her nephews, sons of her brother-father, Oedipus. The terms of kinship become irreversibly equivocal. Is this part of her tragedy? Does this equivocity of kinship lead to fatality?

Antigone is caught in a web of relations that produce no coherent position within kinship. She is not, strictly speaking, outside kinship or, indeed, unintelligible. Her situation can be understood, but only with a certain amount of horror. Kinship is not simply a situation she is in but a set of practices that she also performs, relations that are reinstituted in time precisely through the practice of their repetition. When she buries her brother, it is not simply that she acts from kinship, as if kinship furnishes a principle for action, but that her action is the action of kinship, the performative repetition that reinstates kinship as a public scandal. Kinship is what she repeats through her action; to redeploy a formulation from David Schneider, it is not a form of being but a form of doing.[2] And her action implicates her in an aberrant repetition of a norm, a custom, a convention, not a formal law but a lawlike regulation of culture that operates with its own contingency.

If we recall that for Lacan the symbolic, that set of rules that govern the accession of speech and speakability within culture, is motivated by the father's words, then the father's words are surely upon Antigone; they are, as it were, the medium within which she acts and in whose voice she defends her act. She transmits those words in aberrant form, transmitting them loyally and betraying them by sending them in directions they were never intended to travel. The words are repeated, and their repeatability relies on the deviation that the repetition performs. The aberration that is her speech and her act facilitates such transmissions. Indeed, she is transmitting more than one discourse at once, for the demands that are upon her come from more than one source: her brother also petitions her to give him a decent burial, a demand that in some ways conflicts with the curse that Oedipus has laid upon his son, to die at battle and be received by the underworld. These two demands converge and produce a certain interference in the transmitting of the paternal word. After all, if the father is the brother, then what finally is the difference between them? And what is to elevate the demand of Oedipus over the demand of Polyneices?

The words are upon her, but what does that mean? How does a curse come to inform the action that fulfills the prophecy inherent in the curse? What is the temporality of the curse such that the actions that she takes create an equivocation between the words that are upon her, that she suffers, and the act that she herself performs? How are we to understand the strange *nomos* of the act itself? How does the word of the Other become one's own deed, and what is the temporality of this repetition in which the deed that is produced as a result of the curse is also in some ways an aberrant repetition, one that affirms that the curse produces unanticipated consequences?

Oedipus, of course, unknowingly sleeps with his mother and slays his father, and is driven into the wilderness accompanied by Antigone. In *Oedipus at Colonus* the two of them, along with a small party of followers, are given shelter by Theseus in a land governed by Athens. Oedipus learns that his sons have explicitly forbidden his return to Thebes and also learns that they have turned against one another in a bitter battle for the throne. Toward the end of that play, the second of the trilogy, Polyneices visits Oedipus and calls upon him to return. Oedipus not only refuses but levels a curse against Polyneices, that "you shall never conquer in war your native land; . . . but shall perish by your brother's hand, and kill him who drove you out!" (1385–1393).

Antigone stands by, importuning her father to show benevolence toward Polyneices, and fails. And it remains unclear whether the brother whose act will kill him is Eteocles who delivers the fatal blow, or Oedipus, whose curse both predicts and mandates the blow itself. Polyneices, despite Antigone's protest, decides nevertheless to go into battle with Eteocles, and Antigone is left, crying out "My heart is broken!" She then speaks a line that prefigures her own knowing approach to her own fate: "Brother, how can anyone *not* mourn, seeing you set out to death so clear before you go with open eyes to death!" (Grene 1645–1649). Indeed, Antigone will and—given the chronology of the plays— "already has" undergone precisely the fate she predicts for her brother, to enter death knowingly.

Antigone not only loses her brother to her father's curse, words that quite literally yield the force of annihilation, but she then loses her father to death by the curse that is upon him. Words and deeds become fatally entangled in the familial scene. The acts of Polyneices and Eteocles seem to fulfill and enact the father's words, but his words—and his deeds—are also compelled by a curse upon him, the curse of Laius. Antigone worries over their fate even as she embarks upon her own course of action for which death is a necessary conclusion. Her desire to save her brothers from their fate is overwhelmed, it seems, by her desire to join them in their fate.

Before he dies, Oedipus makes several utterances that assume the status of a curse. He condemns her, but the force of the condemnation is to bind her to him. His words culminate in her own permanent lovelessness, one that is mandated by Oedipus' demand for loyalty, a demand that verges on incestuous possessiveness: "From none did you have love more than from this man, without whom you will now spend the remainder of your life" (1617–1619). His words exert a force in time that exceeds the temporality of their enunciation: they demand that for all time she have no man except for the man who is dead, and though this is a demand, a curse, made *by* Oedipus, who positions himself as her only one, it is clear that she both honors and disobeys this curse as she displaces her love for her father onto her brother. Indeed, she takes her brother to be her only one—she would risk defying the official edict for no kin but Polyneices. Thus she betrays Oedipus even as she fulfills the terms of his curse. She will only love a man who is dead, and hence she will love no man. She obeys his demand, but promiscuously, for he is clearly not the only dead man she loves and, indeed, not the ultimate one. Is the love for the one dissociable from the love for the other? And when it is her "most precious brother" for whom she commits her criminal and honorable act, is it clear that this brother is Polyneices, or could it be Oedipus?

Knowing that he is dying, Oedipus asks, "And will they even shroud my body in Theban soil?" (406) and learns that his crime makes that impossible. He is thus buried by Theseus out of everyone else's sight, including Antigone's. Then, Antigone, in the play by that name, mimes the act of the strong and true Theseus and buries her brother out of sight, making sure that Polyneices' shade is composed of Theban dust. Antigone's assertive burial, which she performs twice, might be understood to be for both, a burial that at once reflects and institutes the equivocation of brother and father. They are, after all, already interchangeable for her, and yet her act reinstitutes and reelaborates that interchangeability.

Although Sophocles wrote *Antigone* several years before *Oedipus at Colonus*, the action that takes place in the former *follows* the action of the latter. What is the significance of this belatedness? Are the words that goad the action understandable only in retrospect? Can the implications of the curse, understood as extended action, be understood only retrospectively? The action predicted by the curse for the future turns out to be an action that has been happening all along, such that the forward movement of time is precisely what is inverted through the temporality of the curse. The curse establishes a temporality for the action it ordains that predates the curse itself. The words bring into the future what has always already been happening.

Antigone is to love no man except the man who is dead, but in some sense she is also a man. And this is also the title that Oedipus bestows upon her, a gift or reward for her loyalty. When Oedipus is banished, Antigone cares for him, and in her loyalty, is referred to as a "man" (*aner*). Indeed, she follows him loyally into the wilderness, but at some point that following imperceptibly turns into a scene in which *she* leads *him*: "Follow, follow me this way with your unseeing steps, father, where I lead you!" (183–184).

Indeed, she is at once cursed with a loyalty to a dead man, a loyalty that makes her manly, compels her to acquire the attribute that carries his approbation such that desire and identification are acutely confounded in a melancholic bind. Oedipus clearly understands gender as something of a curse itself, since one of the ways in which he condemns his sons is by leveling his accusation through the trope of an orientalizing gender inversion:

Those two conform together to the customs that prevail in Egypt in their nature and the nurture of their lives! For there the males sit in their houses working at the loom, and their consorts provide the necessities of life out of doors. And in your case, my children, those who ought to perform this labour sit at home and keep the house like maidens, and you two *in their place* bear the burdens of your unhappy father's sorrows. (337–344, *my emphasis*)

Later, Oedipus maintains that Ismene and Antigone have quite literally taken the place of their brothers, acquiring masculine gender along the way. Addressing his sons, he says:

If I had not begotten these daughters to attend me, I would not be living, for all you did for me. But as it is they preserve me, they are my nurses, they are men, not women, when it comes to working for me; but you are sons of some other, and no sons of mine. (1559–1563)

His daughters thus become his sons, but these same children (Antigone and Ismene), he maintains earlier, are also his "sisters" (328). And so we've arrived at something like kinship trouble at the heart of Sophocles. Antigone has, then, already taken the place of her brother; when she breaks with Ismene, it mirrors the break that Polyneices has made with Eteocles, thus acting, we might say, as brothers do. By the time this drama is done, she has thus taken the place of nearly every man in her family. Is this an effect of the words that are upon her?

Indeed, words exercise a certain power here that is not immediately clear. They act, they exercise performative force of a certain kind, sometimes they are clearly violent in their consequences, as words that either constitute or beget violence. Indeed, sometimes it seems that the words act in illocutionary ways, enacting the very deed that they name in the very moment of the naming. For Hölderlin, this constitutes something of the murderous force of the word in Sophocles. Consider this moment in which the chorus in *Oedipus at Colonus* reminds Oedipus of his crime, a verbal narration *of* the deed that becomes the violent punishment *for* the deed. They not only narrate the events but deliver the accusation, compel his acknowledgment, and inflict a punishment through their interrogatory address:

CHORUS: Unhappy one, what then? You murdered . . . your father?

OEDIPUS: Woe! You have struck me a second blow, anguish upon anguish!

CHORUS: You killed him!

(542–545)

Thus Oedipus is verbally struck by the chorus for having struck and slain his father; the accusation verbally repeats the crime, strikes again where Oedipus is already hurt and where he is thus hurt again. He says, "You strike again," and they strike again, strike with words, repeating, "You killed him"; and the chorus who speaks is ambiguously addressed as "God in heaven," speaking with the force that divine words do. Such scenes no doubt prompted Hölderlin to remark upon the fatality of words in his "Anmerkungen zur Antigone": "The word becomes mediately factic in that it grasps the sensuous body. The tragic Greek word is fatally factic [tödlichfaktisch], because it actually seizes the body that murders."[3]

It is not just that the words kill Oedipus in some linguistic and psychic sense but those words, the ones composing the prior curse of Laius upon him, move him toward incest and murder. In murdering, he fulfills or completes the words that were upon him; his action becomes indissociable from the spoken act, a condition we might say of both the curse that dramatic action reflects and the structure of dramatic action itself. These are words that one transmits, but they are not autonomously generated or maintained by the one who speaks them. They emerge from, in Hölderlin's terms, an inspired or possessed mouth (*aus begeistertem Munde*) and seize the body that murders. They are spoken to Oedipus, but he also restages his trauma, as it were, as his words seize and kill his sons, seize them and make them murderous, and as his words also seize and gender as manly the body of his daughter, Antigone. And they do this precisely by becoming words that act in time, words whose temporality exceeds the scene of their utterance, becoming the desire of those they name, repetitious and conjuring, conferring only retrospectively the sense of a necessary and persistent past that is confirmed by the utterance that predicts it, where prediction becomes the speech act by which an already operative necessity is confirmed.

The relation between word and deed becomes hopelessly entangled in the familial scene, every word transmutes into event or, indeed, "fatal fact," in Hölderlin's phrase. Every deed is the apparent temporal effect of some prior word, instituting the temporality of tragic belatedness, that all that happens has already happened, will come to appear as the always already happening, a word and a deed entangled and extended through time through the force of repetition. Its fatality is, in a sense, to be found in the dynamic of its temporality and its perpetual exile into non-being that marks its distance from any sense of home.[4] According to Hölderlin, this prodigious performativity of the word is tragic both in the sense of fatal and theatrical. Within the theater, the word is acted, the word as deed takes on a specific meaning; the acute performativity of words in this play has everything to do with the words taking place within a play, as acted, as acted out.

There are, of course, other contexts in which words become indissociable from deeds, such as department meetings or family gatherings. The particular force of the word as deed within the family or, more generally, as it circuits within kinship, is enforced as law (*nomos*). But this enforcement does not happen without a reiteration—a wayward, temporal echo—that also puts the law at risk of going off its course.

And if we were to return to psychoanalysis through the figure of Antigone, how might our consideration of this play and this character lay out the possibility of an aberrant future for psychoanalysis, as that mode of analysis becomes appropriated in contexts that could not be anticipated? Psychoanalysis traces the wayward history of such utterances and makes its own lawlike pronouncements along the way. Psychoanalysis might be one mode of interpreting the curse, the apparently predictive force of the word as it bears a psychic history that cannot fully enter narrative form. The encrypted word that carries an irrecoverable history, a history that, by virtue of its very irrecoverability and its enigmatic afterlife in words, bears a force whose origin and end cannot be fully determined.

That the play *Antigone* predates its prehistory, is written decades before *Oedipus at Colonus*, indicates how the curse operates within an uncertain temporality. Uttered before the events, its force is only known retroactively; its force precedes its utterance, as if the utterance paradoxically inaugurates the necessity of its prehistory and of what will come to appear as always already true.

But how surefire is a curse? Is there a way to break it? Or is there, rather, a way in which its own vulnerability might be exposed and exploited? The one who within the present recites the curse or finds oneself in the midst of the word's historical effectivity does not precisely ventriloquize words that are received from a prior source. The words are reiterated, and their force is reenforced. The agency that performs this reiteration knows the curse but misunderstands the moment in which she participates in its transmission.

To what extent is this notion of the curse operating in the conception of a symbolic discourse that is transmitted in certain but unpredictable forms by the speaking subject? And to the extent that the symbolic reiterates a "structural" necessity of kinship, does it relay or perform the curse of kinship itself? In other words, does the structuralist law report on the curse that is upon kinship or does it deliver that curse? Is structuralist kinship the curse that is upon contemporary critical theory as it tries to approach the question of sexual normativity, sociality, and the status of law? And, moreover, if we are seized by this inheritance, is there a way to transmit that curse in aberrant form, exposing its fragility and fracture in the repetition and reinstitution of its terms? Is this breaking from the law that takes place in the reinstituting of the law the condition for articulating a future kinship that exceeds structuralist totality, a poststructuralism of kinship?[5]

The Antigonean revision of psychoanalytic theory might put into question the assumption that the incest taboo legitimates and normalizes kinship based in biological reproduction and the heterosexualization of the family. Although psychoanalysis has often insisted that normalization is invariably disrupted and foiled by what cannot be ordered by regulatory norms, it has rarely addressed the question of how new forms of kinship can and do arise on the basis of the incest taboo. From the presumption that one cannot—or ought not to—choose one's closest family members as one's lovers and marital partners, it does not follow that the bonds of kinship that *are* possible assume any particular form.

To the extent that the incest taboo contains its infraction within itself, it does not simply prohibit incest but rather sustains and cultivates incest as a necessary specter of social dissolution, a specter without which social bonds cannot emerge. Thus the prohibition against incest in the play *Antigone* requires a rethinking of prohibition itself, not merely as a negative or privative operation of power but as one that works precisely through proliferating through displacement the very crime that it bars. The taboo, and its threatening figuration of incest, delineates lines of kinship that harbor incest as their ownmost possibility, establishing "aberration" at the heart of the norm. Indeed, my question is whether it can also become the basis for a socially survivable aberration of kinship in which the norms that govern legitimate and illegitimate modes of kin association might be more radically redrawn.

Antigone says "brother," but does she mean "father"? She asserts her public right to grieve her kin, but how many of her kin does she leave ungrieved? Considering how many are dead in her family, is it possible that mother and father and repudiated sister and other brother are condensed there at the site of the irreproducible brother? What kind of psychoanalytic approach to Antigone's act would foreclose in advance any consideration of overdetermination at the level of the object? This equivocation at the site of the kinship term signals a decidedly postoedipal dilemma, one in which kin positions tend to slide into one another, in which Antigone is the brother, the brother is the father, and in which psychically, linguistically, this is true regardless of whether they are dead or alive; for anyone living in this slide of identifications, their fate will be an uncertain one, living within death, dying within life.

One might simply say in a psychoanalytic spirit that Antigone represents a *perversion* of the law and conclude that the law requires perversion and that, in some dialectical sense, the law is, therefore, perverse. But to establish the structural necessity of perversion to the law is to posit a static relation between the two in which each entails the other and, in that sense, is nothing without the other. This form of negative dialectics produces the satisfaction that the law is *invested* in perversion and that the law is not what it seems to be. It does not help to make possible, however, other forms of social life, inadvertent possibilities produced by the prohibition that come to undermine the conclusion that an invariant social organization of sexuality follows of necessity from the prohibitive law. What happens when the perverse or the impossible emerges in the language of the law and makes its claim precisely there in the sphere of legitimate kinship that depends on its exclusion or pathologization?[6]

In Slavoj Žižek's brief account of Antigone offered in *Enjoy Your Symptom!*,[7] he suggests that Antigone's "no!" to Creon is a feminine and destructive act, one whose negativity leads to her own death. The masculine act is apparently more affirmative for him, the act by which a new order is founded (46). By saying "no" to the sovereign, she excludes herself from the community and is not survivable in that exile. Yet it seems that masculine reparation and building are an effort to cover over that "traumatic rupture" caused by feminine negation. Here it seems that Antigone is once again elevated to a feminine position (unproblematically) and then understood to have constituted the founding negation for the polis, the site of its own traumatic dissolution that the subsequent polity seeks to cover over. But does Antigone simply say "no"? Surely there are negations that riddle her speech, but she also approximates the stubborn will of Creon and circumscribes a rival autonomy by her negation. Later, Žižek will make clear that Antigone counters Creon not with reasons but with a tautology that is nothing other than her brother's name: "The 'law' in the name of which Antigone insists upon Polyneices' right to burial is this law of the 'pure' signifier. . . . It is the Law of the name that fixes our identity" (91–92). But does Antigone call her brother by his name, or does she, at the moment in which she seeks to give him precedence, call him by a kinship term that is, in fact and in principle, interchangeable? Will her brother ever have one name?

What is the contemporary voice that enters into the language of the law to disrupt its univocal workings? Consider that in the situation of blended families, a child says "mother" and might expect more than one individual to respond to the call. Or that, in the case of adoption, a child might say "father" and might mean both the absent phantasm she never knew as well as the one who assumes that place in living memory. The child might mean that at once, or sequentially, or in ways that are not always clearly disarticulated from one another. Or when a young girl comes to be fond of her stepbrother, what dilemma of kinship is she in? For a woman who is a single mother and has her child without a man, is the father still there, a spectral "position" or "place" that remains unfilled, or is there no such "place" or "position"? Is the father absent, or does this child have no father, no position, and no inhabitant? Is this a loss, which assumes the unfulfilled norm, or is it another configuration of primary attachment whose primary loss is not to have a language in which to articulate its terms? And when there are two men or two women who parent, are we to assume that some primary division of gendered roles organizes their psychic places within the scene, so that the empirical contingency of two same-gendered parents is nevertheless straightened out by the presocial psychic place of the Mother and Father into which they enter? Does it make sense on these occasions to insist that there are symbolic positions of Mother and Father that every psyche must accept regardless of the social form that kinship takes? Or is that a way of reinstating a heterosexual organization of parenting at the psychic level that can accommodate all manner of gender variation at the social level? Here it seems that the very division between the psychic or symbolic, on the one hand, and the social, on the other, occasions this pre-emptory normalization of the social field.

I write this, of course, against the background of a substantial legacy of feminist theory that has taken the Lévi-Straussian analytic of kinship as the basis for its own version of structuralist and poststructuralist psychoanalysis and the theorization of a primary sexual difference. It is, of course, one function of the incest taboo to prohibit sexual exchange among kin relations or, rather, to establish kin relations precisely on the basis of those taboos. The question, however, is whether the incest taboo has also been mobilized to *establish* certain forms of kinship as the only intelligible and livable ones. Thus one hears, for instance, the legacy of this tradition in psychoanalysis invoked by psychoanalysts in Paris in recent months against the prospect of "contracts of alliance," construed by conservatives as a bid for gay marriage. Although the rights of gay people to adopt children were not included in the proposed contracts, those who opposed the proposal fear that such contracts might lead to that eventuality and argue that any children raised in a gay family would run the immanent threat of psychosis, as if some structure, necessarily named "Mother" and necessarily named "Father" and established at the level of the symbolic, was a necessary psychic support against an engorgement by the Real. Similarly, Jacques-Alain Miller argued that whereas he was clear that homosexual relations deserve recognition, they should not qualify for marriage because two men together, deprived of the feminine presence, would not be able to bring fidelity to the relationship (a wonderful claim made against the backdrop of our presidential evidence of the binding power of marriage on heterosexual fidelity). Yet other Lacanian practitioners who trace the sources of autism in the "paternal gap" or "absence" similarly predict psychotic consequences for children with lesbian parents.

These views commonly maintain that alternative kinship arrangements attempt to revise psychic structures in ways that lead to tragedy again, figured incessantly as the tragedy of and for the child. No matter what one ultimately thinks of the political value of gay marriage, and I myself am a skeptic here for political reasons I outline elsewhere,[8] the public debate on its legitimacy becomes the occasion for a set of homophobic discourses that must be resisted on independent grounds. Consider that the horror of incest, the moral revulsion it compels in some, is not that far afield from the same horror and revulsion felt toward lesbian and gay sex, and is not unrelated to the intense moral condemnation of voluntary single parenting, or gay parenting, or parenting arrangements with more than two adults involved (practices that can be used as evidence to support a claim to remove a child from the custody of the parent in several states in the United States). These various modes in which the oedipal mandate fails to produce normative family all risk entering into the metonymy of that moralized sexual horror that is perhaps most fundamentally associated with incest.

The abiding assumption of the symbolic, that stable kinship norms support our abiding sense of culture's intelligibility, can be found, of course, outside of the Lacanian discourse. It is invoked in popular culture, by psychiatric "experts" and policy makers to thwart the legal demands of a social movement that threatens to expose the aberration at the heart of the heterosexual norm. It is quite possible to argue in a Lacanian vein that the symbolic place of the mother can be multiply occupied, that it is never identified or identifiable with an individual, and that this is what distinguishes it as symbolic. But why is the symbolic place singular and its inhabitants multiple? Or consider the liberal gesture in which one maintains that the place of the father and the place of the mother are necessary, but hey, anyone of any gender can fill them. The structure is purely formal, its defenders say, but note how its very formalism secures the structure against critical challenge. What are we to make of an inhabitant of the form that brings the form to crisis? If the relation between the inhabitant and the form is arbitrary, it is still structured, and its structure works to domesticate in advance any radical reformulation of kinship.[9]

The figure of Antigone, however, may well compel a reading that challenges that structure, for she does not conform to the symbolic law and she does not prefigure a final restitution of the law. Though entangled in the terms of kinship, she is at the same time outside those norms. Her crime is confounded by the fact that the kinship line from which she descends, and which she transmits, is derived from a paternal position that is already confounded by the manifestly incestuous act that is the condition of her own existence, which makes her brother her father, which begins a narrative in which she occupies, linguistically, every kin position *except* "mother" and occupies them at the expense of the coherence of kinship and gender.

Although not quite a queer heroine, Antigone does emblematize a certain heterosexual fatality that remains to be read. Whereas some might conclude that the tragic fate she suffers is the tragic fate of any and all who would transgress the lines of kinship that confer intelligibility on culture, her example, as it were, gives rise to a contrary sort of critical intervention: What in her act is fatal for heterosexuality in its normative sense? And to what other ways of organizing sexuality might a consideration of that fatality give rise?

Following schools of cultural anthropology inflected by Marxian analysis and Engels's famous study of the origin of the family, a school of feminist anthropologists have taken distance from the Lévi-Straussian model—a critique exemplified perhaps most powerfully by Gayle Rubin,[10] Sylvia Yanagisako, Jane Collier, Michelle Rosaldo,[11] and David Schneider.[12] The critique of the structuralist account, however, is not the end of kinship itself. Understood as a socially alterable set of arrangements that has no cross-cultural structural features that might be fully extracted from its social operations, kinship signifies any number of social arrangements that organize the reproduction of material life, that can include the ritualization of birth and death, that provide bonds of intimate alliance both enduring and breakable, and that regulate sexuality through sanction and taboo. In the 1970s socialist feminists sought to make use of the unwaveringly social analysis of kinship to show that there is no ultimate basis for normative heterosexual monogamous family structure in nature, and we might now add that it has no similar basis in language. Various utopian projects to revamp or eliminate family structure have become important components of the feminist movement and, to some extent, have survived in contemporary queer movements as well, the support for gay marriage notwithstanding.

Consider, for instance, Carol Stack's *All Our Kin* that shows that despite governmental efforts to label fatherless families as dysfunctional, those black urban kinship arrangements constituted by mothers, grandmothers, aunts, sisters, and friends who work together to raise children and reproduce the material conditions of life are extremely functional and would be seriously misdescribed if measured against an Anglo-American standard of familial normalcy.[13] The struggle to legitimate African-American kinship dates back to slavery, of course. And Orlando Patterson's book *Slavery and Social Death* makes the significant point that one of the institutions that slavery annihilated for African-Americans was kinship.[14] The slave-master invariably owned slave families, operating as a patriarch who could rape and coerce the women of the family and effeminize the men; women within slave families were unprotected by their own men, and men were unable to exercise their role in protecting and governing women and children. Although Patterson sometimes makes it seem that the primary offense against kinship was the eradication of paternal rights to women and children within slave families, he nevertheless offers us the important concept of "social death" to describe this aspect of slavery in which slaves are treated as dying within life.

"Social death" is the term Patterson gives to the status of being a living being radically deprived of all rights that are supposed to be accorded to any and all living human beings. What remains uninterrogated in his view, and that I believe resurfaces in his contemporary views on family politics, is precisely his objection to slave men being deprived by slavery of an ostensibly "natural" patriarchal position within the family. Indeed, his use of Hegel supports this point. Angela Davis made a radically different point in *The Black Scholar* several years ago when she underscored the vulnerability of black women to rape both within the institution of slavery and its aftermath, and argued that the family has not served as an adequate protection against sexualized racial violence.[15] Moreover, one can see in the work of Lévi-Strauss the implicit slide between his discussion of kinship groups, referred to as clans, and his subsequent writing on race and history in which the laws that govern the reproduction of a "race" become indissociable from the reproduction of the nation. In these latter writings, he implies that cultures maintain an internal coherence precisely through rules that guarantee their reproduction, and though he does not consider the prohibition of miscegenation, it seems to be presupposed in his description of self-replicating cultures.[16]

The critique of kinship within anthropology has centered on the fiction of bloodlines that work as a presupposition for kinship studies throughout the past century. And yet, the dissolution of kinship studies as an interesting or legitimate field of anthropology does not have to lead to a dismissal of kinship altogether. Kath Weston makes this clear in her book *Families We Choose*, where she replaces the blood tie as the basis for kinship with consensual affiliation.[17] We might see new kinship in other forms as well, ones where consent is less salient than the social organization of need: something like the buddy system that the Gay Men's Health Clinic in New York has established for caring for those who live with HIV and AIDS would similarly qualify as kinship, despite the enormous struggle to gain recognition by legal and medical institutions for the kin status of those relations, manifested for instance by the inability to assume medical responsibility for one another or, indeed, to be permitted to receive and bury the dead.

This perspective of radical kinship, which sought to extend legitimacy to a variety of kinship forms, and which, in fact, refused the reduction of kinship to family, came under criticism by some feminists in the aftermath of the 1960s "sexual revolution," producing, I would suggest, a theoretical conservatism that is currently in tension with contemporary radical sexual politics. It is why, for instance, it would be difficult to find a fruitful engagement at the present time between the new Lacanian formalisms and the radical queer politics of, for example, Michael Warner and friends. The former insists on fundamental notions of sexual difference, which are based on rules that prohibit and regulate sexual exchange, rules we can break only to find ourselves ordered by them anew. The latter calls into question forms of sexual foundationalism that cast viable forms of queer sexual alliance as illegitimate or, indeed, impossible and unlivable. At its extreme, the radical sexual politics turns against psychoanalysis or, rather, its implicit normativity, and the neoformalists turn against queer studies as a "tragically" utopian enterprise.

I remember hearing stories about how radical socialists who refused monogamy and family structure at the beginning of the 1970s ended that decade by filing into psychoanalytic offices and throwing themselves in pain on the analytic couch. And it seemed to me that the turn to psychoanalysis and, in particular, to Lacanian theory was prompted in part by the realization by some of those socialists that there were some constraints on sexual practice that were necessary for psychic survival and that the utopian effort to nullify prohibitions often culminated in excruciating scenes of psychic pain. The subsequent turn to Lacan seemed to be a turn away from a highly constructivist and malleable account of social law informing matters of sexual regulation to one that posits a presocial law, what Juliet Mitchell once called a "primordial law" (something she no longer does), the law of the Father, which sets limits upon the variability of social forms and which, in its most conservative form, mandates an exogamic, heterosexual conclusion to the oedipal drama. That this constraint is understood to be beyond social alteration, indeed, to constitute the condition and limit of all social alterations, indicates something of the theological status it has assumed. And though this position often is quick to claim that although there is a normative conclusion for the oedipal drama, the norm cannot exist without perversion, and only through perversion can the norm be established. We are all supposed to be satisfied with this apparently generous gesture by which the perverse is announced to be essential to the norm. The problem as I see it is that the perverse remains entombed precisely there, as the essential and negative feature of the norm, and the relation between the two remains static, giving way to no rearticulation of the norm itself.

In this light, then, it is perhaps interesting to note that Antigone, who concludes the oedipal drama, fails to produce heterosexual closure for that drama, and that this may intimate the direction for a psychoanalytic theory that takes Antigone as its point of departure. Certainly, she does not achieve another sexuality, one that is *not* heterosexuality, but she does seem to deinstitute heterosexuality by refusing to do what is necessary to stay alive for Haemon, by refusing to become a mother and a wife, by scandalizing the public with her wavering gender, by embracing death as her bridal chamber and identifying her tomb as a "deep dug home" (*kataskaphes oikesis*). If the love toward which she moves as she moves toward death is a love for her brother and thus, ambiguously, her father, it is also a love that can only be consummated by its obliteration, which is no consummation at all. As the bridal chamber is refused in life and pursued in death, it takes on a metaphorical status and, as metaphor, its conventional meaning is transmuted into a decidedly nonconventional one. If the tomb is the bridal chamber, and the tomb is chosen over marriage, then the tomb stands for the very destruction of marriage, and the term "bridal chamber" (*numpheion*) represents precisely the negation of its own possibility. The word destroys its object. In referring to the institution it names, the word performs the destruction of the institution. Is this not the operation of ambivalence in language that calls into question Antigone's sovereign control of her actions?

Although Hegel claims that Antigone acts with no unconscious, perhaps hers is an unconscious that leaves its trace in a different form, indeed that becomes readable precisely in her travails of referentiality. Her naming practice, for instance, ends up undoing its own ostensible aims. When she claims that she acts according to a law that gives her most precious brother precedence, and she appears to mean "Polyneices" by that description, she means more than she intends, for that brother could be Oedipus and it could be Eteocles, and there is nothing in the nomenclature of kinship that can successfully restrict its scope of referentiality to the single person, Polyneices. The chorus at one point seeks to remind her that she has more than one brother, but she continues to insist on the singularity and non-reproducibility of this term of kinship. In effect, she seeks to restrict the reproducibility of the word "brother" and to link it exclusively to the person of Polyneices, but she can do this only by displaying incoherence and inconsistency.[18] The term continues to refer to those others she would exclude from its sphere of application, and she cannot reduce the nomenclature of kinship to nominalism. Her own language exceeds and defeats her stated desire, thereby manifesting something of what is beyond her intention, of what belongs to the particular fate that desire suffers in language. Thus she is unable to capture the radical singularity of her brother through a term that, by definition, must be transposable and reproducible in order to signify at all. Language thus disperses the desire she seeks to bind to him, cursing her, as it were, with a promiscuity she cannot contain.

In this way Antigone does not achieve the effect of sovereignty she apparently seeks, and her action is not fully conscious. She is propelled by the words that are upon her, words of her father's that condemn the children of Oedipus to a life that ought not to have been lived. Between life and death, she is already living in the tomb prior to any banishment there. Her punishment precedes her crime, and her crime becomes the occasion for its literalization.

How do we understand this strange place of being between life and death, of speaking precisely from that vacillating boundary? If she is dead in some sense and yet speaks, she is precisely the one with no place who nevertheless seeks to claim one within speech, the unintelligible as it emerges within the intelligible, a position within kinship that is no position.

Although Antigone tries to capture kinship through a language that defies the transposability of the terms of kinship, her language loses its consistency—but the force of her claim is not therefore lost. The incest taboo did not work to foreclose the love that it should have between Oedipus and Jocasta, and it is arguably faltering again for Antigone. The condemnation follows Oedipus' act and his recognition, but for Antigone, the condemnation works as foreclosure, ruling out from the start any life and love she might have had.

When the incest taboo works *in this sense* to foreclose a love that is not incestuous, what is produced is a shadowy realm of love, a love that persists in spite of its foreclosure in an ontologically suspended mode. What emerges is a melancholia that attends living and loving outside the livable and outside the field of love, where the lack of institutional sanction forces language into perpetual catachresis, showing not only how a term can continue to signify outside its conventional constraints but also how that shadowy form of signification takes its toll on a life by depriving it of its sense of ontological certainty and durability within a publicly constituted political sphere.

To accept those norms as coextensive with cultural intelligibility is to accept a doctrine that becomes the very instrument by which this melancholia is produced and reproduced at a cultural level. And it is overcome, in part, precisely through the repeated scandal by which the unspeakable nevertheless makes itself heard through borrowing and exploiting the very terms that are meant to enforce its silence.

Do we say that families that do not approximate the norm but mirror the norm in some apparently derivative way are poor copies, or do we accept that the ideality of the norm is undone precisely through the complexity of its instantiation? For those relations that are denied legitimacy, or that demand new terms of legitimation, are neither dead nor alive, figuring the nonhuman at the border of the human. And it is not simply that these are relations that cannot be honored, cannot be openly acknowledged, and cannot therefore by publicly grieved, but that these relations involve persons who are also restricted in the very act of grieving, who are denied the power to confer legitimacy on loss. In this play, at least, Antigone's kin are condemned prior to her crime, and the condemnation she receives repeats and amplifies the condemnation that animates her actions. How does one grieve from within the presumption of criminality, from within the presumption that one's acts are invariably and fatally criminal?

Consider that Antigone is trying to grieve, to grieve openly, publicly, under conditions in which grief is explicitly prohibited by an edict, an edict that assumes the criminality of grieving Polyneices and names as criminal anyone who would call the authority of that edict into question. She is one for whom open grieving is itself a crime. But is she guilty only because of the words that are upon her, words that come from elsewhere, or has she also sought to destroy and repudiate the very bonds of kinship that she now claims entitlement to grieve? She is grieving her brother, but part of what remains unspoken in that grief is the grief she has for her father and, indeed, her other brother. Her mother remains almost fully unspeakable, and there is hardly a trace of grief for her sister, Ismene, whom she has explicitly repudiated. The "brother" is no singular place for her, though it may well be that all her brothers (Oedipus, Polyneices, Eteocles) are condensed at the exposed body of Polyneices, an exposure she seeks to cover, a nakedness she would rather not see or have seen. The edict demands that the dead body remain exposed and ungrieved, and though Antigone seeks to overcome the edict, it is not entirely clear all of what she grieves or whether the public act she performs can be the site of its resolution. She calls her loss her brother, Polyneices, insists on his singularity, but that very insistence is suspect. Thus her insistence on the singularity of her brother, his radical irreproducibility, is belied by the mourning she fails to perform for her two other brothers, the ones she fails to reproduce publicly for us. Here it appears that the prohibition against mourning is not simply imposed upon her but is enjoined independently without direct pressure by public law.

Her melancholia, if we can call it that, seems to consist in this refusal to grieve that is accomplished through the very public terms by which she insists on her right to grieve. Her claim to entitlement may well be the sign of a melancholia at work in her speech. Her loud proclamations of grief presuppose a domain of the ungrievable. The insistence on public grieving is what moves her away from feminine gender into hubris, into that distinctively manly excess that makes the guards, the chorus, and Creon wonder: Who is the man here? There seem to be some spectral men here, ones that Antigone herself inhabits, the brothers whose place she has taken and whose place she transforms in the taking. The melancholic, Freud tell us, registers his or her "plaint," levels a juridical claim, where the language becomes the event of the grievance, where, emerging from the unspeakable, language carries a violence that brings it to the limits of speakability.

We might ask what remains unspeakable here, not in order to produce speech that will fill the gap but to ask about the convergence of social prohibition and melancholia, how the condemnations under which one lives turn into repudiations that one performs, and how the grievances that emerge against the public law also constitute conflicted efforts to overcome the muted rage of one's own repudiations. In confronting the unspeakable in *Antigone*, are we confronting a socially instituted foreclosure of the intelligible, a socially instituted melancholia in which the unintelligible life emerges in language as a living body might be interred into a tomb?

Indeed, Giorgio Agamben has remarked that we live increasingly in a time in which populations without full citizenship exist within states; their ontological status as legal subjects is suspended. These are not lives that are being genocidally destroyed, but neither are they being entered into the life of the legitimate community in which standards of recognition permit for an attainment of humanness.[19] How are we to understand this realm, what Hannah Arendt described as the "shadowy realm," which haunts the public sphere, which is precluded from the public constitution of the human, but which is human in an apparently catachrestic sense of that term?[20] Indeed, how are we to grasp this dilemma of language that emerges when "human" takes on that doubled sense, the normative one based on radical exclusion and the one that emerges in the sphere of the excluded, not negated, not dead, perhaps slowly dying, yes, surely dying from a lack of recognition, dying, indeed, from the premature circumscription of the norms by which recognition as human can be conferred, a recognition without which the human cannot come into being but must remain on the far side of being, as what does not quite qualify as that which is and can be? Is this not a melancholy of the public sphere?

Arendt, of course, problematically distinguished the public and the private, arguing that in classical Greece the former alone was the sphere of the political, that the latter was mute, violent, and based on the despotic power of the patriarch. Of course, she did not explain how there might be a prepolitical despotism, or how the "political" must be expanded to describe the status of a population of the less than human, those who were not permitted into the interlocutory scene of the public sphere where the human is constituted through words and deeds and most forcefully constituted when its word becomes its deed. What she failed to read in *The Human Condition* was precisely the way in which the boundaries of the public and political sphere were secured through the production of a constitutive outside. And what she did not explain was the mediating link that kinship provided between the public and private spheres. The slaves, women, and children, all those who were not property-holding males were not permitted into the public sphere in which the human was constituted through its linguistic deeds. Kinship and slavery thus condition the public sphere of the human and remain outside its terms. But is that the end of the story?

Who then is Antigone within such a scene, and what are we to make of her words, words that become dramatic events, performative acts? She is not of the human but speaks in its language. Prohibited from action, she nevertheless acts, and her act is hardly a simple assimilation to an existing norm. And in acting, as one who has no right to act, she upsets the vocabulary of kinship that is a precondition of the human, implicitly raising the question for us of what those preconditions really must be. She speaks within the language of entitlement from which she is excluded, participating in the language of the claim with which no final identification is possible. If she is human, then the human has entered into catachresis: we no longer know its proper usage. And to the extent that she occupies the language that can never belong to her, she functions as a chiasm within the vocabulary of political norms. If kinship is the precondition of the human, then Antigone is the occasion for a new field of the human, achieved through political catachresis, the one that happens when the less than human speaks as human, when gender is displaced, and kinship founders on its own founding laws. She acts, she speaks, she becomes one for whom the speech act is a fatal crime, but this fatality exceeds her life and enters the discourse of intelligibility as its own promising fatality, the social form of its aberrant, unprecedented future.

Notes

1. ANTIGONE'S CLAIM

1. See Luce Irigaray, "The Eternal Irony of the Community," in *Speculum of the Other Woman*, trans. Gillian Gill (Ithaca: Cornell University Press, 1985); "The Universal as Mediation" and "The Female Gender," in *Sexes and Genealogies*, trans. Gillian Gill (New York: Columbia University Press, 1993); "An Ethics of Sexual Difference," in *An Ethics of Sexual Difference*, trans. Carolyn Burke and Gillian Gill (London: The Athlone Press, 1993).

2. My text will not consider the figure of "Antigone" in Greek myth or in other classical or modern tragedies. The figure I refer to here is restricted to her textual appearance in Sophocles' *Antigone*, *Oedipus at Colonus* and, obliquely, in *Oedipus Tyrannus*. For a nearly exhaustive treatment of the figure of Antigone, see George Steiner, *Antigones* (reprint, New Haven: Yale University Press, 1996).

3. See Patricia Mills, ed., *Feminist Interpretations of Hegel* (College Park: Pennsylvania State University Press, 1996), especially Mills's own contribution to that volume. See also Carol Jacobs, "Dusting Antigone" (*MLN* 3, no. 5 [1996]: 890–917), an excellent essay on Antigone that

engages Irigaray's readings of *Antigone* and shows the impossibility of representation marked by the figure of Antigone.

4. G. W. F. Hegel, *The Phenomenology of Spirit*, trans. A. V. Miller (London: Oxford University Press, 1977), pp. 266ff. All further citations will be from this text and from the German: *Phänomenologie des Geistes. Werke* 3 (Frankfurt: Suhrkamp Verlag, 1970).

5. Jacques Lacan, *The Seminar of Jacques Lacan, Book VII: The Ethics of Psychoanalysis, 1959–60*, ed. Jacques-Alain Miller, trans. Dennis Porter (New York: Norton, 1992), pp. 243–90.

6. Kaja Silverman is distinctive among Lacanian theorists for insisting that the law of kinship and the law of speech ought to be considered separable from one another. See Kaja Silverman, *Male Subjectivity at the Margins* (New York: Routledge, 1992).

7. For an interesting discussion of how audience identification can shift in relation to the play, see Mark Griffith, "Introduction," *Sophocles Antigone* (Cambridge: Cambridge University Press, 1999), pp. 58–66.

8. Here it should become clear that I am in substantial agreement with Peter Euben's claim that "the polarities between household and city, nature and culture, woman and man, *eros* and reason, divine and human law are no more persuasive as an interpretive scaffold from the standpoint of the characterization of Antigone than they [are] from the standpoint of Creon"; see Peter Euben, "Antigone and the Languages of Politics," in *Corrupting Youth: Political Education, Democratic Culture, and Political Theory* (Princeton: Princeton University Press, 1997), p. 170. Over and against this view, see Victor Ehrenberg, *Sophocles and Pericles* (Oxford: Basil Blackwell, 1954), pp. 28–34. Antigone is only criminal to the extent that she occupies one tension within an ambiguous sense of law. Jean-Pierre Vernant and Pierre Vidal-Naquet argue that "neither of the two religious attitudes set forth in the *Antigone* can by itself be the right one unless it grants to the other the place that is its due, unless it recognizes the very thing that limits and competes with it"; see "Tensions and Ambiguities in Greek Tragedy," in *Myth and Tragedy in Ancient Greece*, trans. Janet Lloyd (New York: Zone Books, 1990), p. 41.

9. For a very interesting article that establishes a psychoanalytic frame-

work for considering Antigone's incestuous attachments, see Patricia J. Johnson, "Woman's Third Face: A Psychosocial Reconsideration of Sophocles' *Antigone*," in *Arethusa* 30 (1997): 369–398.

10. For a structuralist reading of the play that assumes a constant opposition between Creon and Antigone, see Charles Segal, *Interpreting Greek Tragedy: Myth, Poetry, Text* (Ithaca: Cornell University Press, 1986).

11. Froma Zeitlin offers important insight into the problem of burial in *Antigone* and *Oedipus at Colonus*, arguing that in the former, Creon effectively blurs the line between life and death that the act of burial is supposed to delineate. "Kreon's refusal of burial," she writes, "offends against the entire cultural order, . . . but can also be construed as an offense against time itself" (152). For Zeitlin, Antigone overvalues death and blurs the distinction between life and death from another perspective. Insightfully, she argues that "Antigone's longing for death before her time is also a regression to hidden sources of the family from which she springs" (153). See Froma Zeitlin, "Thebes: Theatre of Self and Society," reprinted in John J. Winkler and Froma Zeitlin, *Nothing to do with Dionysos? Athenian Drama in its Social Context* (Princeton: Princeton University Press, 1990), pp. 150–167.

12. Nicole Loraux points out that mourning is not only women's task but one that is ideally performed inside the boundaries of the home. When women's mourning becomes public, a loss of self is threatened for the civic order. For her brief but insightful remarks on burial in Antigone, see Nicole Loraux, *Mothers in Mourning*, trans. Corinne Pache (Ithaca: Cornell University Press, 1998), pp. 25–27, 62–64. See also by Loraux "La main d'Antigone," *Métis* 1 (1986): 1994–1995.

13. For an excellent discussion of the place and style of performative speech in public discourse in Athens, see Josiah Ober, *The Athenian Revolution: Essays On Ancient Greek Democracy and Political Theory* (Princeton: Princeton University Press, 1996), especially chapters 3 and 4. For a wonderful and insightful essay on the performative in *Antigone*, see Timothy Gould, "The Unhappy Performative," in *Performativity and Performance*, eds. Andrew Parker and Eve Kosovsky Sedgwick (New York: Routledge, 1995), pp. 19–44.

14. Hegel approaches the question of Antigone in three separate discussions and does not always maintain a consistent discussion of the significance of the play: in *The Phenomenology of Spirit*, which forms the focus of the discussion here and in chapter 2 of this text; in *The Philosophy of Right*, where he argues that the family must exist in a reciprocal relation with the state; and scattered in various places in the *Aesthetics* but focused in volume 2, in the final section on "Poetry," under the subsection, "The Concrete Development of Dramatic Poetry and its Genres." In this last context he argues that both Creon and Antigone constitute tragic figures, "in the power of what they are fighting." Unlike the largely elliptical discussion of Antigone in *The Phenomenology of Spirit*, in which Antigone is superseded by Creon, here they are positioned in a relationship of reciprocal tragedy: "There is immanent in both Antigone and Creon something that in their own way they attack, so that they are gripped and shattered by something intrinsic to their own actual being." Hegel concludes this discussion with extreme praise for the play: "The *Antigone* seems to me to be the most magnificent and satisfying work of art of this kind." See Hegel's *Aesthetics: Lectures on Fine Art, Volume II*, trans. T. M. Knox (Oxford: Clarendon Press, 1975), pp. 1217–1218.

In an essay, "The Woman in White: On the Reception of Hegel's 'Antigone'" (*The Owl of Minerva* 21, no. 1 [Fall 1989]: 65–89), Martin Donougho argues that the Hegelian reading of Antigone was the most influential nineteenth-century reading, countered perhaps most forcefully by Goethe who wrote of his skeptical views in his letters to Eckermann. There Goethe called into question whether the tension between family and state was central to the play and suggested that the incestuous relation between Antigone and Polyneices was hardly the exemplar of the "ethical" (71).

15. Of course, women were not citizens in classical Athens, even though the civic culture was imbued with valences of femininity. For a very useful discussion of this paradox, see Nicole Loraux, *The Children of Athena: Athenian Ideas About Citizenship and the Division Between the Sexes*, trans. Caroline Levine (Princeton: Princeton University Press, 1993).

16. Claude Lévi-Strauss, *The Elementary Structures of Kinship*, ed. Rodney Needham, trans. James Harle Bell and John Richard Von Sturmer (Boston: Beacon Press, 1969); *Les Structures élémentaires de la parenté* (Paris: Mouton, 1967). Citations in the text refer first to the English pagination and then to the French.

17. For a cursory but shrewd critique of the nature/culture distinction in relation to the incest taboo, which proves to be at once foundational and unthinkable, see Jacques Derrida, "Structure, Sign, and Play," in *Writing and Difference*, trans. Alan Bass (Chicago: University of Chicago Press, 1978), especially pp. 282–284.

18. See also George Steiner's brief discussion of incestuous sibling bonds from 1780 to 1914 in *Antigones*, pp. 12–15.

19. Martha C. Nussbaum, *The Fragility of Goodness: Luck and Ethics in Greek Tragedy and Philosophy* (Cambridge: Cambridge University Press, 1986), p. 59. For a stronger, anti-psychoanalytic argument against interpreting the Antigone-Polyneices relationship as an incestuous bond, see Vernant and Vidal-Naquet, "Oedipus Without the Complex," in *Myth and Tragedy in Ancient Greece*, pp. 100–102.

20. Dylan Evans, *An Introductory Dictionary of Lacanian Psychoanalysis* (London: Routledge, 1996), p. 202.

21. Juliet Mitchell, *Psychoanalysis and Feminism* (New York: Random House, 1974), p. 370.

22. For an interesting history of the symbolic and a controversial account of symbolic positions of sex within contemporary kinship arrangements, see Michel Tort, "Artifices du père," *Dialogue: Recherches cliniques et sociologiques sur le couple et la famille* 104 (1989): 46–60; "Symboliser le Différend," *Psychanalystes* 33 (1989): 9–18; and "Le Nom du père incertain: Rapport pour le ministère de la justice" (unpublished, on file with the author).

23. See Robert Graves, *The Greek Myths: 2* (London: Penguin, 1960), p. 380. I am grateful to Carol Jacobs's article cited above for this last reference.

24. See Seth Bernardete, "A Reading of Sophocles's *Antigone I*," *Interpretation: Journal of Political Philosophy* 4, no. 3 (1975): 156. Bernardete here

cites Wilamowitz-Moellendorf, *Aischylos Interpretationen* 92, no. 3, to support his translation. Stathis Gourgouris offers the following provocative comments on "the rich polyvalence of Antigone's name":

> The preposition *anti* means both "in opposition to" and "in compensation of "; *gonē* belongs in a line of derivatives of *genos* (kin, lineage, descent) and means simultaneously offspring, generation, womb, seed, birth. On the basis of this etymological polyphony (the battle for meaning at the nucleus of the name itself), we can argue that Antigone embodies both an opposition of kinship to the polis (in compensation for its defeat by the *demos* reforms), as well as an opposition *to* kinship, expressed by her attachment to a sibling by means of a disruptive desire, *philia* beyond kinship.

From the chapter "Philosophy's Need for Antigone," in Stathis Gourgouris, *Literature as Theory (for an Antimythical Era)* (Stanford: Stanford University Press, forthcoming).

2. Unwritten Laws, Aberrant Transmissions

1. Political commentators on the play such as Jean Bethke Ehlstain have suggested that Antigone represents civil society, that her relation with Haemon and the chorus, in particular, represents a "voice" that is neither that of kinship nor of the state. There is, clearly, a community judgment that is expressed by the chorus, but it would be a mistake to thereby conclude that the community operates as a separate or separable sphere from either kinship or the state. My view is that there is no uncontaminated voice with which Antigone speaks. This means that she can neither represent the feminine over and against the state nor can she represent a version of kinship in its distinction from state power. See Jean Bethke Ehlstain, "Antigone's Daughters," in *Democracy* 2, no. 2 (April 1982): 46–59. Seyla Benhabib traces the ambivalence in Hegel's understanding of women, arguing that Antigone finally has no place in the dialectical advancement of universality. This is clearly true in *The Phe-*

nomenology of Spirit and seems also to follow from the oppositions maintained with *The Philosophy of Right*, as Benhabib shows. But it would be interesting to consider in this regard Hegel's claim in the *Aesthetics* that Antigone's universality is to be found in her "pathos." See *Hegel's Aesthetics: Lectures on Fine Art, Volume I*, trans. T. M. Knox (Oxford: Clarendon Press, 1975), p. 232. For her discussion, see Seyla Benhabib, *Situating the Self: Gender, Community, and Postmodernism in Contemporary Ethics* (New York: Routledge, 1992) pp. 242–259. On this topic, also see Valerie Hartouni, "Antigone's Dilemmas: A Problem of Political Membership," *Hypatia* 1, no. 1 (Spring 1986): 3–20; Mary Dietz, "Citizenship with a Feminist Face," *Political Theory* 13, no. 1 (1985): 19–37.

2. All citations are from the Miller translation cited in note 4, chapter 1, with reference to the Suhrkamp German edition cited in the same note. Citations refer first to the English pagination and then to the German.

3. See Charles Taylor, *Hegel and Modern Society* (Cambridge: Cambridge University Press, 1979), pp. 1–68.

4. Derrida points out that Hegel generalizes too quickly from the specific situation of Antigone's family to the more general "law" she is said to represent and to defend. After all, she can hardly be representing the living and intact family, and it is unclear what structures of kinship she represents. Derrida writes, "And what if the orphanage were a structure of the unconscious? Antigone's parents are not some parents among others. She is the daughter of Oedipus and, according to most of the versions from which all the tragedians take their inspiration, of Jocasta, of her incestuous grandmother. Hegel never speaks of this generation moreover [de plus], as if it were foreign to the elementary structures of kinship." Although in what follows, he seems to concur with Hegel on the desireless status of her relation to her brother, he may be writing ironically, since he both negates the desire but then also calls it an impossible desire, affirming it as a desire of sorts: "Like Hegel, we have been fascinated by Antigone, by this unbelievable relationship, this powerful liaison without desire, this immense, impossible desire that could not live, capable only of overturning, paralyzing, or exceeding any system and history, of interrupting the life of the concept, of cutting off its breath. " See Jacques

Derrida, *Glas*, trans. John P. Leavey Jr. and Richard Rand (Lincoln: University of Nebraska, 1986), pp. 165–166.

5. Hegel cites from the Hölderlin translation of Sophocles' *Antigone* as *Antigonä* (Frankfurt: Wilmans Verlag, 1804), three years prior to the publication of the *Phenomenology*.

6. Grene, *Antigone*.

7. Hegel proceeds to talk about the doer who makes such an acknowledgment, but it appears that this doer cannot be Antigone. He refers instead to Polyneices and Eteocles, two brothers who are described as contingently emerging from "Nature," each of whom claims an equal right to lead the community. "Human law in its universal existence is the community, in its activity in general is the manhood of the community, in its real and effective activity is the government. It *is, moves*, and *maintains* itself by consuming and absorbing into itself the separateness of the Penates [household gods], or the separation into separate families presided over by womankind, and by keeping them dissolved in the fluid continuity of its own nature" (287–288).

8. "The worth of the son lies in his being lord and master of the mother who bore him, and of the brother as being one in whom the sister finds man on a level of equality, that of the youth as being one through whom the daughter . . . obtains the enjoyment and dignity of wifehood [den Genuss und die Würde der Frauenschaft erlangt]" (288, 353).

9. [Das Gemeinwesen kann sich aber nur durch Unterdrückung dieses Geistes der Einzelheit erhalten.] He also acknowledges that the community requires this very individualism and so "creates it" [weil es wesentliches Moment ist, *erzeugt es* ihn zwar ebenso] (288, 353, emphasis mine). This simultaneous creation and suppression takes place through the operation of what he calls a "repressive attitude [*unterdrückende Haltung*]," one which animates its object as a hostile principle. Thus it becomes unclear whether Antigone herself is hostile, or whether she is enjoined to be hostile precisely by this repressive attitude. In any event, she is cast as "evil and futile" precisely because of her separation from the universal.

10. "The negativity prominent in war . . . preserves the whole" (289).

11. There he writes that "man has his actual substantive life in the state" and that "woman . . . has her substantive destiny in the family and to be imbued with family piety is her ethical frame of mind." See *Hegel's Philosophy of Right*, trans. T. M. Knox (London: Oxford University Press, 1967), p. 114. He takes Sophocles' *Antigone* to be one of the most "sublime presentations of this virtue," an interpretation, by the way, that Lacan will find to be utterly wrong. This "law of woman," for Hegel, is the "law of a substantiality at once subjective and on the plane of feeling, the law of the inward life, a life which has not yet attained its full actualization." It is referred to as "the law of the ancient gods, 'the gods of the underworld,'" "an everlasting law, and *no man knows at what time it was first put forth*" (115, my emphasis).

12. *Hegel's Philosophy of Right.* "This is the supreme opposition in ethics and therefore in tragedy; and it is individualized in the same play in the opposing natures of man and woman" (115).

13. Jacques Lacan, *Le Séminaire, Livre II: Le Moi dans la théorie de Freud et dans la technique de la psychanalyse, 1954–1955* (Paris: Éditions du Seuil, 1978), p. 42; *The Seminar of Jacques Lacan, Book II: The Ego in Freud's Theory and in the Technique of Psychoanalysis, 1954–1955*, ed. Jacques-Alain Miller, trans. Sylvana Tomaselli (New York: Norton, 1988), p. 29.

14. [Il y a un circuit symbolique extérieur au sujet, le petit cercle qu'on appelle son destin, est indéfiniment inclus.] *Le Séminaire II*, 123.

15. "This is nothing more nor less than what is presupposed by the unconscious such as we discover and manipulate it in analysis" (*Seminar II*, 30). Here it is not simply that the symbolic functions *like* the unconscious but that the symbolic is precisely what the unconscious presupposes.

16. *Le Séminaire, Livre VII: L'éthique de la psychanalyse* (Paris: Éditions du Seuil, 1986); *The Seminar of Jacques Lacan, Book VII: The Ethics of Psychoanalysis*, ed. Jacques-Alain Miller, trans. Dennis Porter (New York: Norton, 1992).

17. "Il désigne la limite que la vie humaine ne saurait trop longtemps franchir"(*Le Séminaire II*, 305).

18. And it is language that confers being on him: "Antigone appears
. . . as a pure and simple relationship of the human being to that of which
he miraculously happens to be the bearer, namely, *the signifying cut* that
confers on him the indomitable power of being what he is in the face of
everything that may oppose him" (*Seminar VII*, p. 282, my emphasis).

19. Orlando Patterson, *Slavery and Social Death* (Cambridge: Harvard
University Press, 1982), pp. 38–46.

3. PROMISCUOUS OBEDIENCE

1. Steiner, *Antigones*, p. 18.

2. David Schneider, *A Critique of the Study of Kinship* (Ann Arbor:
University of Michigan Press, 1984), p. 131.

3. "Das Wort mittelbarer faktisch wird, indem es den sinnlicheren
Körper ergreift. Das griechischtragische Wort ist tödlichfaktisch, weil der
Leib, den es ergreift, wirklich tötet," in "Anmerkungen zur Antigone" in
Friedrich Hölderlin, Werke in einem Band (Munich: Hanser Verlag, 1990),
p. 64. All English citations are from "Remarks on Antigone," *Friedrich
Hölderlin: Essays and Letters*, ed. and trans. Thomas Pfau (Albany: State
University of New York Press, 1977). See also Philippe Lacoue-Labarthe,
Métaphrasis suivi de la théâtre de Hölderlin (Paris: Presses Universitaires de
France, 1988), pp. 63–73.

4. Heidegger offers a sustained meditation on Hölderlin's translation
of *Antigone* (1803), as well as his "Remarks on Antigone" with respect to
the various ways that Hölderlin brings forward Antigone's "uncanni-
ness." The proximity to death underscored in the "Remarks on Antigone"
corresponds in large measure to Heidegger's reading of Antigone as one
whose exile from the hearth establishes her essential relation to a sense of
being that is beyond human life. This participation in what is non-living
turns out to be something like the condition of living itself. As in the
reading supplied by Jacques Lacan, Heidegger also claims that
"[Antigone] names being itself" (118), and that this proximity to being

involves a necessary estrangement from living beings even as it is the ground of their very emergence.

Similarly, Heidegger understands the "unwritten law" to which Antigone refers as a relationship to being and to death:

> Antigone assumes as what is fitting that which is destined to her from the realm of whatever prevails beyond the higher gods (Zeus) and beyond the lower gods. . . . Yet this refers neither to the dead, nor to her blood-relationship with her brother. What determines Antigone is that which first bestows ground and necessity upon the distinction of the dead and the priority of blood. What that is, Antigone, and that also means the poet, leaves without a name. Death and human being, human being and embodied life (blood) in each case belong together. "Death" and "blood" in each case name different and extreme realms of human being.

From Martin Heidegger, *Hölderlin's Hymn "The Ister"*, trans. William McNeill and Julia Davis (Bloomington: Indiana University Press, 1996), p. 117.

5. There have been several important works within anthropology in the last few decades showing the limitations of structuralist paradigms for thinking the problem of kinship, including Marilyn Strathern, *Reproducing the Future: Essays on Anthropology, Kinship, and the New Reproductive Technologies* (New York: Routledge, 1992). In *Gender and Kinship: Essays Toward a Unified Analysis*, ed. Jane Fishburne Collier and Sylvia Junko Yanagisako (Stanford: Stanford University Press, 1987), the editors argue against a view of kinship that focuses exclusively on symbolic relations at the expense of social action. Perspectives in that volume that seek to elaborate the complex social conditions of kinship relations against both functionalist and purely structuralist accounts are to be found in the important contributions by John Comaroff, Rayna Rapp, Marilyn Strathern, and Maurice Bloch. See also Sylvia Junko Yanagisako, "The Analysis of Kinship Change," in *Transforming the Past: Tradition and Kinship Among Japanese Americans* (Stanford: Stanford University Press,

1985), where she faults both structuralist and functionalist accounts for failing to give a dynamic understanding of kin relations. David Schneider, in *A Critique of the Study of Kinship*, elaborates how the theoretical models of kinship elaborated by Fortes, Leach, and Lévi-Strauss impose theoretical constraints on ethnographic perception, failing to account for societies that failed to approximate the theoretical norm and that, regardless of their claim not to take biological relations of reproduction as the point of departure of kinship study, still make that assumption operate as a fundamental premise of their work (see pp. 3–9, 133–177). In particular, the work of Pierre Clastres in France made dramatically and vociferously, clearly drawing in part on the prior work of Marshall Sahlins, argues that the sphere of the social could not be reduced to the workings of kinship, and cautions against any effort to treat kinship rules as supplying the principles of intelligibility for any social order. He writes, for instance, that it is not possible to reduce relations of power to those of exchange: "Power relates . . . to the . . . essential structural levels of society: that is, it is at the very heart of the communicative universe" (37). In *Society Against the State*, trans. Robert Hurley (New York: Zone, 1987), pp. 27–49, Clastres argues for relocating the "exchange of women" within relations of power. And in "Marxists And Their Anthropology," he offers a searing criticism of Maurice Godelier on the matter of kinship and the state. There he argues that the principle function of kinship is not to institute the incest taboo nor to exemplify relations of production, but to transmit and reproduce the "name" of the relative, and that "the function of nomination, inscribed in kinship, determines the entire sociopolitical being of primitive society. It is there that the tie between kinship and society is located." See Pierre Clastres, *Archaeology of Violence*, trans. Jeanine Herman (New York: Semiotext(e), 1994), p. 134.

For a notion of kinship as embodied practice, see also Pierre Bourdieu, *The Logic of Practice*, trans. Richard Nice (Stanford: Stanford University Press, 1990), pp. 34–35.

6. Here I am not suggesting that the perverse simply inhabits the norm as something that remains autonomous, but neither am I suggest-

ing that it is dialectically assimilated into the norm itself. It might be understood to signal the impossibility of maintaining a sovereign lock on any claim to legitimacy, since the reiteration of the claim outside of its legitimated site of enunciation shows that the legitimate site is not the source of its effectivity. Here I am indebted to what I take to be Homi Bhabha's significant reformulation dispersed throughout his work of both speech act theory and the Foucaultian notion of discourse developed in the latter's *Archaeology of Knowledge*.

7. Slavoj Žižek, *Enjoy Your Symptom!* (New York: Routledge, 1992).

8. See my contribution, "Competing Universalities," to Judith Butler, Ernesto Laclau, and Slavoj Žižek, *Universality, Hegemony, Contingency* (London: Verso, 2000).

9. It has been one strategy here to argue that the incest taboo does not always produce normative family, but it is perhaps more important to realize that the normative family that it does produce is not always what it seems. There is, for instance, clearly merit in the analysis offered by Linda Alcoff and others that heterosexual incest within heterosexually normative families is an extension rather than abrogation of patriarchal prerogative within heterosexual normativity. Prohibition is not fully or exclusively privative, that is, just as prohibition requires *and produces* the specter of crime it bars. And for Alcoff, in an interesting Foucaultian move, the prohibition offers the cover that protects and abets the practice of incest. But is there any reason to check the productivity of the incest taboo here, at this dialectical inversion of its aim? See Linda Alcoff, "Survivor Discourse: Transgression or Recuperation?" SIGNS 18, no. 2 (Winter 1993): 260–291. See also for a very interesting and brave Foucaultian discussion of the criminalization of incest, Vikki Bell, *Interrogating Incest: Feminism, Foucault, and the Law* (London: Routledge, 1993).

10. Gayle Rubin, "The Traffic in Women: Notes on the 'Political Economy' of Sex," in *Toward an Anthropology of Women*, ed. Rayna R. Reiter (New York: Monthly Review Press, 1975).

11. See *Gender and Kinship*, ed. Collier and Yanagisako. For an excellent critique of gender-based approaches to kinship, which shows how

the uncritical presumption of marriage underwrites the anthropological approach to kinship, see John Borneman, "Until Death Do Us Part: Marriage/Death in Anthropological Discourse," *American Ethnologist* 23, no. 2 (1996): 215–238.

12. David Schneider, *A Critique of the Study of Kinship; American Kinship* (Chicago: University of Chicago Press, 1980).

13. Carol Stack, *All Our Kin: Strategies for Survival in a Black Community* (New York: Harper and Row, 1974).

14. See, in particular, the very interesting use of Hegel in his discussion of the dehumanization in slavery in Orlando Patterson, *Slavery and Social Death: A Comparative Study*, pp. 97–101. For Patterson's illuminating discussion of Antigone, see *Freedom, Volume 1: Freedom in the Making of Western Culture* (New York: Basic Books, 1991), pp. 106–132.

15. Angela Davis, "Rape, Racism, and the Myth of the Black Rapist," reprinted in *Women, Race, and Class* (New York: Random House, 1981), pp. 172–201.

16. Claude Lévi-Strauss, *Race et Histoire* (Paris: Denoël, 1987); *Structural Anthropology, Volume* 2, trans. Monique Layton (New York: Basic Books, 1974), pp. 323–362.

17. Kath Weston, *Families We Choose: Lesbians, Gays, Kinship* (New York: Columbia University Press, 1991).

18. Like Lacan, Derrida appears to accept the singularity of Antigone's relationship to her brother, one that Hegel describes, as we have already seen, as a relationship without desire. Although Derrida does not read the play, *Antigone*, in *Glas*, he does read the figure of Antigone in Hegel, working within the terms of that reading to show how Antigone comes to mark the radical outside to Hegel's own systematic thinking and Hegel's own "fascination by a figure inadmissable within the system" (151). Although I agree that neither the figure nor the play of Antigone cannot be readily assimilated into either the framework of *The Phenomenology of Spirit* or the *The Philosophy of Right*, and is curiously applauded in the *Aesthetics* as "the most magnificent and appeasing work of art," it would be a mistake to take her persistent unreadability within the Hegelian perspective as a sign of her final or necessary unreadability.

19. Giorgio Agamben, *Homo Sacer: Sovereign Power and Bare Life*, trans. Daniel Heller-Roazen (Stanford: Stanford University Press, 1998).

20. Hannah Arendt, *The Human Condition* (Chicago: University of Chicago Press, 1969), part 1.

Index